BUMPING INTO GOD

A Search for the Sound of Spirit

Will Schmit

Bumping into God

A Search for the Sound of Spirit

Copyright © 2022 Will Schmit
All rights reserved.

Permission for use of all interviews contained in this publication were given to the author and are on file with the publisher.

Scripture taken from the New King James Version®, (NKJV). Copyright © 1982 by Thomas Nelson. Used by permission. All rights reserved.

Scripture quotations marked (NIV) are taken from the Holy Bible, New International Version®, NIV® Copyright © 1973, 1978, 1984, 2011 by Biblica, Inc.™ Used by permission of Zondervan. All rights reserved worldwide. www.zondervan.com The "NIV" and "New International Version" are trademarks registered in the United States patent and Trademark Office by Biblica, Inc.™

Scripture quotations marked MSG are taken from THE MESSAGE, copyright © 1993, 2002, 2018 by Eugene H. Peterson. Used by permission of NavPress. All rights reserved. Represented by Tyndale House Publishers, Inc.

Holy Bible, New Living Translation, copyright © 1996, 2004, 2015 by Tyndale House Foundation. Used by permission of Tyndale House Publishers, Inc., Carol Stream, Illinois 60188. All rights reserved.

Scripture quotations are from The Holy Bible, English Standard Version (ESV), copyright © 2001 by Crossway Bibles, a publishing ministry of Good News Publishers. Used by permission. All rights reserved.

Cover Photos: Justin Grimaldo Sightseer Productions
Cover Designer: Robin Black

Publisher's Cataloging-in-Publication data
Name: Schmit, Will
Title: Bumping Into God
Subtitle: A Search for the Sound of Spirit/ by Will Schmit
Identifiers: LCCN: 2022903325
ISBN 978-1-953114-59-4
Subjects: 1. MUS054000 Music/Philosophy & Social Aspects
2. OCC019000 / Body, Mind, Spirit / Inspiration & Personal Growth

Published by EA Books Publishing a division of
Living Parables of Central Florida, Inc. a 501c3
EABooksPublishing.com

DEDICATION

This book is dedicated to the loving memory and legacy of my Maestro Tony Pagano who taught me the colors of music are anything but black and white and my scat singing Pastor Donald Wesley. These are the giants in my life who dared me to stand tall and sit still.

CONTENTS

Dedication	iii
Acknowledgements	v
Chapter 1 – Sound Check	1
Chapter 2 – Music Theory	29
Chapter 3 – The Sax Camp Interviews	47
Chapter 4 – Praise Raises More Than an Eyebrow	79
Chapter 5 – Taking Notes Seriously	167
Chapter 6 – Brighter Moments	175
Chapter 7 – Have I Mentioned My Mentor?	213
Chapter 8 – Coda	227
Endnotes	239
Also by the Author	241

ACKNOWLEDGMENTS

Bumping into God wouldn't be possible without the support and contribution of all the musicians who gave such patient responses to my curious inquiries into their personal examples of improvisation and community as an inexplicable but tangible source of creativity in excess of preparation and skill.

Learning to listen and listening to learn are of course related attitudes but until we meet someone who employs the practice we sometimes believe progress and insight are mysterious, otherworldly realms available only to the exceptional talented.

The following too-short-list of people did not let any such rules or notions stand in the way of encouraging me to write, play, pray, or live my life within ear shot of the Most High.

Thank you Jerry Wimmer for giving me my first saxophone, Ashbolt Stewart for teaching me the clave`, Geo Howard for filling in my dream of being a rock star, Bobby Orvis for turning me on to jazz, Josef Brinkmann for his globe circling compassion and general hipness and my Mom Virginia Adeline

Remmel-Schmit for dancing in the kitchen, singing to the coffee pot and taking her place with the angels watching over me.

BUMPING INTO GOD

A Search for the Sound of Spirit

Will Schmit

CHAPTER 1

Sound Check

♪♪♪

I was nervous. The clock on the wall tapped out sixty beats per minute. Sixty BPM seemed like a racing speed on the metronome anytime I tried to practice my saxophone; now it ticked like a swinging Sword of Damocles over my head.

Audition night for a new band in a new town. In my previous band I had been the front man, the vocalist . . . well, the speaker might be a better term, as I didn't sing. We set poetry to music, and I was the poet. The players in that band were well trained, talented, and accomplished improvisers. They made me look and sound good at the same time as they inadvertently demoralized me, because as a very amateur musician, I couldn't hope to match them in proficiency.

That band broke up right after our first recording was released, leaving me free to pursue the dream of playing in tune, and in time, on my own. My progress was set up against my enthusiasm to make beautiful sounds on my horn. I had some instruction. I had been advised to aim for a tone steady and long enough to reach around the whole world and come back to me as a heart line to and from the ear of God. This made sense to me back in the '70s. Making sense was important.

My decades of woodshedding helped me get my horn out of the case, and around my neck. I took a deep inhalation and entered the keyboard player's studio. He was looking to form a new group to bring "semi-sacred" music into the local bar scene. The small talk of introductions didn't give me confidence. I knew I was faking it. I played my soprano like it was cymbal in a drum kit, adding an accent here and there, a little shimmering color, a tremolo seated in the fear that my trembling lip would squeak volumes.

We finished the song and my host asked me if I could make an upcoming gig and maybe try out a few ideas. To play without fainting was the first idea that came to mind and the second one was no poetry. I didn't want that persona to get in the limelight again. It was time for purification. Time to test the theory that we could express love, common sense, and compassion without words. As this experiment was in the bright brass buckle of the Bible belt, the other concern was how we could come across as Christian, and not just spiritual, if we didn't announce our faith or use visual aids.

The issue was never resolved. I caved in and did a couple of poems and eventually quit the group. We didn't rehearse, and I proved myself too old, and not talented enough, to be satisfied jazzing up old hymns for the reveling crowd of two seated tables and one lone tipsy gypsy dancer at the beach bar in the next town that "hired" us to play for donations and free coffee.

What remained in my spiritual gig bag from that brief collaboration was the question of how to credit the Source of the sound of many waters rushing.

Famous world class musicians like John Coltrane, Carlos Santana, and Ravi Shankar could claim the Holy Spirit as their different drummer and most people would tap their feet in approval, but what about the rest of us?

"The Little Drummer Boy" gets airtime in December, and we *rum-pum-pun* around the cookies on the table with the notion that we can dedicate our music to the Lord, even if we play spoons. So far so good, but that doesn't translate into scales, tempos, and technique as the realm of operation.

Sun Ra and his Infinite Intergalactic Arkestra travelled the Space Waves in search of a beat that wasn't just universal but was the universe itself. What he found is long out of print and perhaps can best be explained by the time I saw him live at an outdoor festival and got caught in the crush of the crowd. Folks in the front row, left over from a Dixieland band's set, were rushing to get away, while the new comers to the scene were clamoring to get up close.

Playing with God as the rhythm section of our faith is a deeper vein than mere dedication. "This song goes out to Jesus," can be as sincere as the singer makes it, but Jesus coming through the speakers as a still, small voice is something else altogether. If David, the warrior king of Israel, were alive today he might post "singer/songwriter" on his Facebook page. What he did with his harp strings carried the way of the Lord as much as what he did with a slingshot.

When lovers sing a serenade, the hope is that beauty will come to the window. We sometimes act as if our heroic music is a vehicle to invite God to look on us with favor, but it may well be that we are the ones on the balcony, listening to the song of all hearts. The prayer of Saint Francis asks the Lord to make us instruments of His peace. I wonder if playing a musical instrument might make us more susceptible to His perspective, like some sort of lightening rod of love?

I was in my twenties when I acquired my first saxophone. It was a high school band hand-me-down from my college roommate. If there was anything spiritual about the gift, it was lost in the basement echoes of me puffing my cheeks and moving my fingers. I remember the C scale seeming to be an insurmountable mountain as my pinkie reached for the low note. The valley of the shadow of death cast it's pall a few sessions later when I began reaching, now with both pinkies, for the signature note of the tenor saxophone, the low B flat.

The moaning that came out of my horn gave me the glimmer of connection to cultures and emotions I never imagined, let alone encountered in my white suburban upbringing. I might have been berating stubborn camels in the desert, or communing with breaching whales in the high seas; either way I was a long way from Kansas or from playing anything that might resemble a tune.

As sometimes happens, even in ordinary odysseys, I was directed to a teacher at the local music conservatory who took one look at my rig and tossed my mouthpiece in a trashcan. He charged me fifty dollars to replace it with one of his own. Several years passed before I realized what a favor installing me with an Otto Link Star 5 Signature mouthpiece turned out to be, so forgive me if I seem slow to perceive God's hand in precipitating events.

The Maestro, Tony Pagano, drew three notes on a sheet of music paper. I remember one of them was A flat, requiring another pinkie maneuver. I made a machine gun series of notes, squinting my eyebrows together to show I was serious. Tony drew another set of three notes, which I sensed all his other students had recognized as a chord. For me it was another invitation to exhaust myself, for at least a minute, blowing what may have been the actual notes he wrote down.

He admitted that we would have to take a different direction in instruction and had me sit forward so my ear was level with his horn's bell. Tony played every note possible on the horn, and quite a few I was sure are impossible, with the goal of setting the sound, the physical vibration, in my inner ear. The phrase "rang true" rattled around in my skull as Tony's tones filled the microscopic spaces between the bones in my head. To demonstrate the intensity of my desire to play I formed a habit of squeezing my eyebrows together in concentration. To illustrate the obvious, Tony put his finger on my forehead to point out no air was escaping from that part of my thick skull. Producing my sound would be a matter of coordinating my mouth and throat with intentional breathing, and relaxed, deliberate fingering. As I was already a few decades older than most beginning music students, he was curious about my motivation to begin studying the saxophone. I told him I listened to John Coltrane records, and although it was the most profound musical listening experience imaginable, it drove my roommate nuts and he gave me his old horn to wean me from my fascination.

The lesson ended. Tony invited me back for a second session and asked me to pay particular attention to any music I heard in my dreams. He mentioned that he got the call to play jazz when, as an underage lad, he had snuck into a club to hear Charlie Parker. The proprietor of the place had put him in the front row, under a table, where to his amazement, Tony watched the notes come out of Parker's horn like colors of streaking clouds. Tony's father, a strict Sicilian marching band musician, would have none of that "race music" in his house, relegating the pull to jazz to an undercurrent of Tony's classical training.

As for my Lawrence Welk-infused upbringing, when it was my turn to take music lessons, the family sold the piano. I have a memory of bicycle chains being added to the piano's strings to create a honky tonk sound, but I may have just been dreaming between very white Christmases. My high school's policy, and I doubt that it was unique, was that you couldn't be both an athlete and a musician, as they met during the same extra-curricular time slots and thus cancelled each other out. I ran for the cross country team after the football coach found me on the scales at 117 pounds in the guise of his defensive tackle, and the closest I got to musical expression was performing mouth percussion with an upper class teammate mile after mile ahead of the rest of the team.

A few years later this same classmate, Bobbie Orvis, by then a college sophisticate, introduced me to his collection of jazz LPs. I instantly understood that while rock and roll may never grow old—and I would point to the Rolling Stones touring in their '70s or KISS tribute bands playing at a casino near you as evidence of that—jazz was for mature audiences only.

The levels of intricate musical skill and exchange of exploratory expression between instruments suddenly explained why God left so much room between the stars.

The two major philosophical points of rock and roll, i.e. "Brown Shoes Don't Make It," from Frank Zappa and "Love is All You Need," from the Beatles created a nutshell that couldn't begin to contain a Max Roach solo on a high hat, or Rahsaan Roland Kirk playing three instruments at once. I found out that America had a serious underbelly of exultation that had nothing to do with long-haired boys in tights grinding their groins to a back beat of amplified four counts. In short, I became an obnoxious jazz purist and spent every green-back as fast as I could on an iconic collection of jazz records with the frenzy of an archeologist on the trail of King Tut's golden slippers.

Listening to music, however important, is not the same as playing an instrument. The instrument I chose, which I sometimes imagine actually chose me, required stamina, strength, and skill that only came through deliberate steps. And the first step is producing a legitimate long tone. Just one. A single sound that the metronome might measure as a bit of eternity at the same time the neck muscles and lower back begin to realize there's an opportunity for serious damage. The lowest note in a monotone can easily be misdiagnosed as monotony until the player recognizes what lock this key of Zen-like precision and persistence is designed to open.

I began collecting anecdotes of the great players to find day-to-day examples of a musician's life to which I might hitch my shooting star. Sonny Rollins took a very famous sabbatical from public performing to practice under the bridges of New York. I found a local highway embankment and began bouncing my long, low tones off the concrete buttress in a ritualistic attempt to join a community I wasn't quite sure I'd be able to negotiate on talent. The rush of overhead traffic sure made it easier to get loud and the setting gave my labors the sense of being industrious.

The process of isolating yourself to practice is known in jazz parlance as "woodshedding." I didn't have access to an actual shed, but just a short walk from my day job was an historical preserved round barn atop one of California's golden hills. Lunch breaks would find me inside the barn exploring the particular acoustic differences of playing in a wooden circular environment. I'm not sure what musical progress I was making, but spiritually, playing in orthodox amphitheaters was setting my stage for God, as no one else was around I thought might be interested in listening to my sounds.

To paraphrase Coltrane's great poem, *A Love Supreme*, "It all has to do with God . . . thoughts-deeds-vibrations, all go back to God and He cleanses all." Coltrane's legacy as a musician was fortified by his mystic experience of kicking heroin cold turkey in his mother's house. His father and grandfather were Christian ministers, and although Coltrane's finest recordings exhibited the influence of Eastern cultures (and what didn't during the mid-'60s), his exquisite recording, "Father Son and Holy Ghost, " gave tribute to his church roots. In my typical throw-out-the-baby-with-the-bathwater enthusiasm I sometimes considered John Coltrane as a more influential set of JC initials than Jesus Christ.

I was raised Catholic and had an underlying conviction that every commercially acceptable presentation of Jesus was so short of the mark as to be laughable, but Coltrane's example gave me a divine thread to weave my hope around until I had a more tangible God encounter for myself. I chased a few gurus around the country, paid the established fees to have my chakras tickled, learned to sit still, or bow, in front of altars of flowers. I drew the line at smudging sage because playing at being entitled to Indigenous culture seemed to be an insult to the people who actually paid those dues, though it might have been the bad drumming that wilted my enthrallment.

I knew I was engaged with God, as I had the gift of receiving poems whole, and more or less intact, out of the blue. Blue being the color of Mary's robes (remember I'm Catholic), I took the friendly skies and parting clouds as evidence I was being chosen, even if I was a bit foggy on Who was the Chooser. My passport to the realm of creative people was stamped by the positive reception of my poetry performances and publications, but I still carried my self-inflicted martyr's weight of not being good enough as a musician to play standards in a jazz combo.

Tony invited me to the club where he was playing to sit in with his band. To make things easier for me, he instructed the rhythm section to play "rhythm changes," which is a universal strategy among musician to play the chord changes to the tune, "I Got Rhythm" and allow the soloist to freely improvise over the vamp.

Had I known what "rhythm changes" actually meant, this would have been a sound suggestion on my maestro's part, however I interpreted his instruction as meaning I should play in different rhythms, maybe spend a little time in a 4/4 beat, then switch to a 3/4, or a 6/8. If I had known how to do that, I may have earned some respect with the band or audience. However, since I didn't know the changes or how to affect any variations in time, I just began blowing and squawking until, one by one, the band members stopped playing behind me. Tony finally came and put his hand on my shoulder to get me to quit.

"You play with such energy," he told me, "if you could just channel it into music, it would be really something."

Seeking musical solace, I began jamming with other illiterate musicians intent on making grooves through the study of adding and subtracting. Some sessions satisfied but none of them ratified the trial-and-error method as a sure-footed way to climb any particular musical mountains.

I kept coming back to Tony, who eventually taught me how to play in all twelve keys and how to interpret a jazz chart. I say interpret, rather than read, as I couldn't quite yet read music. Tony liked to muse about how much more universal the language of music might become if we were all encouraged to speak/sing, read, and write it as if it were our native tongue. It saddened him to observe music as the only language in the world that fewer people can write than read. The myth that musical instruction is only for gifted and talented students irked him to no end. That may been why he was so patient with me, the poster child of the unschooled-but-willing spirit.

By now I had friends who were legitimate working musicians. When I moved to California, to escape Wisconsin's wind chill factor, I landed in the living room of the bass player Jerry Wimmer, who had given me my first saxophone. His band was a rock and reggae group with some regular followers. As I fell into the culture, I shifted my creative focus to poetry, all but shedding my connection to the horn like a snakeskin on a Texas highway.

The drummer of the group, Ashbolt Stewart, shared my love of jazz and encouraged me to keep my lip up. I went to jazz concerts and workshops with him in the San Francisco area, including an Art Blakey concert, which was recorded live at the Keystone Korner jazz club. We got there early and prepared to step inside the club by adjusting our attitudes in the alleyway next to the stage door.

I soon had to rub my eyes to make sure I wasn't seeing things because coming up the sidewalk was my maestro, Tony Pagano, whom I hadn't seen in four years. He had driven non-stop from Milwaukee to San Francisco, using his wiper blades as a constant metronome to keep him awake and focused. Naturally the concert was sold out and supernaturally, Ashbolt had an extra ticket.

I began to take lessons again, got a much better horn, and went to every jazz concert I could afford: Dexter Gordon, Max Roach, Charlie Mingus, Keith Jarrett, Pharoah Sanders, Don Cherry, Charlie Haden, Airto Moreira, Dewey Redman, and later his son Joshua, McCoy Tyner, Rahsaan Roland Kirk, Archie Shepp. Heroes. Icons. I was among the clouds, witnessing American improvisational music's most noteworthy contributors.

I eventually got so bold as to enroll in the local junior college's big band class. The first day I sat it the front row with the other horns and realized these kids had been playing since they were babies. The teacher handed out what seemed like enormous charts and counted off the downbeat. I made not a sound as the music sped by me like a bullet train on a greased track. The teacher made some mention of some rests in bar 16 and moved onto the next song. This one ended in a group crescendo, and I was able to flutter a few middle Cs and Ds hoping I was blending into the chorus.

At the break the teacher asked what I thought of the class so far, and I expressed my rampant enthusiasm, "Just think what it will be like when I can read music."

"Yeah, just think," was his metered reply.

I enrolled in sight-reading classes, a small group combo, took the rhythm-only studio labs like it was part of the breakfast of champions and by the end of the semester was able to play a set with the big band in concert and perform a 12-bar solo, in time and in tune, for . . . 11 bars.

At the peak of my prowess I just stopped playing. It was too much work to get good. Tony had moved to France. My wife at the time suggested I give up the horn and focus on poetry, my "actual" talent. The horn might've gone into a pawnshop, I might've sold it—I'm not sure what happened. If I had more cognition of the wheels of time I might have said I was taking a sabbatical. I might've believed it. Believing was precisely the problem. I had to find God.

My makeshift worship of whatever intrigued me at the time couldn't hold my interest any better than the ankle I broke falling off a twenty-foot cliff could support my body weight. I was flat on my back, recuperating on pain pills plus when I had a dream of entering Saint Peter's gate. Since I was raised Catholic, I expected good things to happen, but when I got closer, Peter pulled a bar from the gate and whomped me on the head. I rolled into a ball on the ground and he continued to beat me like a snare drum.

He was yelling at me like only Saint Peter could, "We gave you the gift of telling stories and sent you down there and what did you come back with? Nothing! *(Thud)* Nothing! *(Thwack)* Nothing! *(Thump)*."

I woke up white-knuckling the sheets of my bed in sweat and began searching my body for bruises. My body had no marks, but I knew I was a marked man. All the junk mail from my week of bed rest was piled up next to me. Thus inspired, I crawled out to a desk for scissors and glue stick and began to snip my way through the advertisements and circulars to make story poems in the great tradition of cut out ransom notes.

The technology of the day allowed me to make xeroxed copies, which added a black and white legitimacy to my cartoonish creations. I added a few inches to my poetic legacy by randomly stapling them to telephone poles around town. You would've done the same thing in my shoes, once the swelling went down. As soon as I assembled a few dozen collages, I had a showing in an art gallery and sold a half a dozen "originals" for $7 each, which helped me publish a book of poems, punctuated by cut outs.

I came back to the creative fold like an origami swan returning to a lake of summer dreams. I booked readings in coffee shops, sold my poetry books out of the taxi I drove for a living, did a few guest spots on local radio, and got my picture in the cultural section of the local papers. What more could a poet want, except maybe a band?

I had friends who played percussion in an African dance class. They had been patiently helping me click two sticks together to make a clave beat. I invited them to the house to experiment with perhaps putting my poetry to music. As what I used to call luck—but now know it to be the hand of God—

would have it, a great friend of mine, and fellow student of Tony Pagano, Jim Glynn, was in town and volunteered to be our spontaneous audience.

Jim was a well-respected jazz DJ in my hometown, and he was considering moving to a larger network in Portland. He rolled his wheelchair into the only spot in the living room that wasn't filled with instruments and smiled his made-for-radio smile.

"Well, let's hear what you got."

Congas, bass, accordion, and bags full of hand percussion instruments set a mood for me to tell a poetic story about "The People I Trust," the title piece of a book of poetry I had recently published. "If He were born today, what would that little Nazarene boy want for Christmas ?" was the general theme of the piece. Without knowing the direction we were heading, we made a poetic, musical foray into the world of geo-political propaganda, with the emphatic threat to wash people's mouths out with hope.

We had a hit. Our style of collaboration sometimes began with me bringing a poem to the group to be set to music; sometimes the band brought a groove they thought would lend itself to lyricism. When it worked, it was as if we had rehearsed the number for years. When it didn't work, it was like pushing rocks uphill in wet socks, but something was afoot. We thought it was magical, but knew it was grace. The sum of the parts added up to more than the whole.

Irreverent reverence was the hook we cast into the sea of coffeehouse venues to see what might catch on. We named ourselves, Wiley Jadavega, (my nom-de-plume) and The Poetry Section after discovering the largest bookstore in town actually had no poetry section. Find a need and fill it—the basic marketing principle that brought the world sticky notes and easy-light charcoal had birthed a spoken-word multi-instrumental confab of percolating percussion and poetic profundity with a special nod to fun and ditties.

The band had a good small market run. We did live radio, recorded an album, got featured in the local cultural section of the newspaper, built a fan club of several hundred people, sold T-shirts, and packed the best coffee houses every few weeks for two years. For my birthday, my older brother paid to have the band's logo tattooed on my forearm, forever commemorating our storied arc from niche to cliché.

The flaw in the anointment was my ego. My sole purpose was a bit of stardom for being able to seduce an audience. I was too sexy for my too many hats, which ultimately led to divorce, sobriety and a retreat from the public eye. Coltrane's advice to "Keep your eye on God," began to take on literal and literary meaning as, in the grand scheme of things, there really isn't much else worth looking at. I entered the rooms of 12-step programs and found to my delight I could walk with Jesus and still keep my leather jacket.

♫ ♫ ♫

I re-married to a saint in the making who had grown up in dance studios, and I limited my writing to personal love poems and poignant inscriptions on greeting cards. My new bride bought me two beautiful saxophones. I began to wade in the waters of becoming a real musician by taking lessons from Al Garth, who played with the Eagles, and Steve Wolf who toured the world with a contemporary reincarnation of Duke Ellington's band.

My bride, Trey, and I began attending a black gospel church, The House of Refuge Christian Fellowship. Trey was soon recruited into singing with the praise team, and I sort of muscled my horn into the church's ministerial visits to San Quentin State Prison. I approached the prison chapel's bandstand with the expectation of the band members taking me aside to walk through the song list so I could appropriate some plausible and timely licks. No such luck. The inmates walked to their instruments and, before I could count to one, launched into a full fury of funky drop-down-to-the-ground and reach-for-the-sky crescendo to back the thirty-man choir raising the roof from behind the podium.

The brother manning the soundboard noticed he couldn't hear my horn, although he didn't notice it was because I wasn't playing. He came over between songs and set the microphone into the bell of my horn. I began praying the most sincere prayer of my fledgling born-again life along the lines of, "God if you're real don't let me embarrass myself."

I moved over to the keyboard player to see if I could read the black keys he was playing to find out what key we were in, but he had a cheat button on his keyboard allowing him to modulate using only the white keys, so he was no help at all. I was alone and amplified, which is to say terrified, when the music started. Somehow I found a call-and-response groove to the choir. I not only had a place to stand up in the music, but the notes coming out of my horn made me feel as if I had uncovered a fulcrum point from which to move the world.

God had taken over my fingers. There was no other explanation for it. I was playing so far above my ability that both my pastor and my wife turned around to see who had taken control of my horn. I had been delivered. Not only was my eye on God, but also my ears, as well, as I poured out a solo that had the congregation shouting and my band mates grinning as if they knew all along that all things are possible with God.

The possibilities, folks say, are endless, but the beginnings are usually deep secrets testing the surface. My head, just above the water line of faith, began to stir with the prospect of playing music at least as well as I wrote poetry. I still had my original notes from the early days of instruction with Tony. As my willingness increased, another teacher, or two, would manifest long enough to discredit this or that alibi for my not improving. Some combination of practical shyness and inhibition kept me in the woodshed, with occasional forays to play solo for whatever inmates I was visiting at the time as a volunteer minister.

We moved from California to North Carolina, and despite a church, or two being on every corner, my playing in a worship band on Sundays never took root. I attributed it to not knowing enough about the style of music being played, but years later a particularly encouraging, but likely delusional, friend of mine suggested God wanted to keep my music to Himself until I was ready to represent Him. I always went back to Coltrane: "A Love Supreme." Pedal on the A-flat and hold your head high.

One Sunday, I was high in the mountains of Kenyan coffee country on a mission trip with my local church. Holding my horn high above my head was the only way to keep it from clogging from the rising dust of the dancing congregation's dirt floor. We had been escorted the last quarter mile or so to the village church by the village throng, complete with tree branches and squealing children. The road to the village, as vertical as a lightning bolt, gave out around 7,000 feet, so we suburban Americans unpacked the vehicles and, in our Sunday best, trekked to the church. We were careful to step over the wires that ran from the bicycle-powered generator to the chapel sound system.

In the States, few of my fellow travelers had ever been to a black church, segregation still being the unspoken norm of American Christianity, so the foot-stomping, body-swaying celebration was a cultural shift as much as it was a spiritual revelation. We were on a mission from God, and with *The Blues Brothers* movie as a reference point, we fell into the worship service clapping in time to the interpreters who were trying to match the widest smiles in the universe. The soundman was busy switching the wires from the keyboard to the guitar player because their power source couldn't support both when I unpacked my tenor and stepped up to sway into the fray.

I could've played half of "Mary Had A Little Lamb," and it would've made no difference to the enthusiasm of the event. I found out later that my saxophone was the first the locals had ever seen. In fact, the people in our little group were the first white people some of the church-goer's kids had ever come across. I thought the young man rubbing my tattoo of the Lion of Judah was trying to determine if the ink was permanent, but it may have been more a test to see if my skin was real.

The rhythm section was hammering on round metal gears of some abandoned machine. As the red earth rose in gusts of unity, I saw myself, as if from heaven's window, fulfilling my call to life's highest stage. I may never execute a jazz standard with any competency in public, but for a Wisconsin rube to play in an African church with the joy of the Lord as the conducting energy . . . that seemed enough of a pinnacle to hold in place til the Angel Gabriel calls for the coda. The Lord and I apparently had a covenant I knew little about. Scripture says as we delight ourselves in the Lord, He will grant us the desires of our heart, even if that desire requires more than talent, discipline, instruction, and travelling halfway around the world. It requires trust.

CHAPTER TWO

Music Theory

♪♪♪

Camaraderie and community often express the "something larger than the sum of its parts" phenomenon. This sense of hyper-connectivity may be an unspoken reason why music, especially jazz and praise music, draws our attention away from ourselves into our selves.

Naturally we are first pulled into the sound and pulse of the song, and then perhaps our focus may shift to the personalities and talents producing the music. Occasionally, our inner hearing begins to ask about the orchestrator of our very breath and heartbeat. The singer, "took our breath away," the drummer matched, and even exceeded, the pounding in our chest until we say, "My heart stood still."

The art of articulating the holy, of revealing, and reveling, in raucous reverence, is a combination of underlying and overlapping themes. The fascinating unity of Creator and creation is reflected in our being able to identify a musician by his or her sound. We judge them by their fruit: ripe, delicious, hanging on a tender branch in the dawn-lit dew. A note comes out of the horn and the heart of the player transfers the conception, perception, and resounding perspective to the recipient. The listener listens in.

The Lord, sometimes, gets credit for inspiring such interaction. The word *inspire* breaks down pretty well into "in spirit."

"A little bird told me" is a widely understood explanation for a sudden transfer of insight or information. A jazz enthusiast might cite Jimmy Heath, one of the greatest embodiments of jazz culture, as being THE "Little Bird" in question. A Christian devotee might source the Dove of Peace. Is it important to give it a name? Can we acknowledge that sometimes music causes, or should I say *pauses*, us to hear something ringing in ourselves that originates in the literal, aural pulse of the cosmos?

Jazz asks questions of the Creator by coaxing intimate solutions of the complex and spontaneous juxtapositions of shared, but very personal experiences. The player who draws attention to himself may have a technician's prowess of his (sic) instrument, but he is missing the spirit of jazz. We call it playing music, but the interplay among musicians takes a lot of work. Beautiful music succeeds as musicians disguise the strenuous reality of preparation, practice, rehearsal, and painstaking precision that goes into being perceived as effortless expression.

I heard Joshua Redman speak of the serious joy and visceral potency of playing live with an engaged audience participating in slicing pieces of a mysteriously universal pie. He credits the honesty of the moment as being a lubricant to the engine of growth that encourages the player, and the audience, to deal with it night after night. The live in the living room jam session was a part of his upbringing and that stirred up feeling of extended family is the sensation Joshua seeks in his recordings and performances.

In the 1980s, Horace Silver moved to create his own recording label to feature five albums of healing, holistic music. He was concerned that being so forward with a spiritual basis for music might damage his "secular" career. His concern proved to be accurate, so his project folded into obscurity. I would love to get my hands—and ears—on those recordings. Mr. Silver would be one composer I would trust to explore the qualities of the God who gives God-given talents. The phraseology of the Black-gospel-swinging church almost reduces the call and response of a hand-clapping, side-stepping choir to a clichéd soundtrack. However, the profundity and impact of even the simplest spiritual is of such historical importance that it tips the scales, especially the blue ones, towards eternal consequence.

One particular song, out of hundreds with a similar theme, is "Gotta Serve Somebody." The lyrics tell us we have to serve someone, whether it is the devil or God. The song spells out the lay of the promised and the present land (if Bob Dylan really wrote that lick, my yarmulke is once again off to him). The problem I have with stopping short of assigning

Personhood to Spirituality is that it leaves the creative spark in a nebulae of nebulous origin with no prospect of progress or relationship. But, hey, that's me—well, me and the Apostle Paul, who spoke in the book of Romans about the practice of worshipping the creation in lieu of the Creator.

God is incapable of making us wary of Him, even in the context of the fear (awe equaling acknowledgement) of the Lord being the beginning of wisdom. So the apprehension, the misgiving that creative people sometimes exhibit about the Creator having a Master Plan, to quote Pharoah Sanders, must stem for how God is presented by His proponents here on earth. Like the bumper sticker says, "Lord, protect me from Your followers!" Jesus Himself asked His day-to-day disciples if they were "yet so dull" when they asked if not observing certain dietary customs might defile a man.

To be plain, in fact blunt, Jesus explained that it is not what goes into a person, but what comes out of that person's heart that might defile or degrade him or her. In our day, we might push the question to another extreme and ask if heroin, oxycodone, or methamphetamine devour a soul as much as attitudes of racism or polarizing political patronizing. This heart of the matter is where music delves. In some hearts, the testimony emerges that the music, indeed, plays the musician more so than the other way around.

Does that mean the fingers, the ears, and the lungs operate at a different pace, a different level of attentiveness and appreciation? An accepted evaluation of Thelonius Monk is that he, in his body, was the primary instrument, and he used the piano as a device to release the sounds he found inside of him. Gary Bartz, the alto saxophonist, who among his other credits, played with Miles Davis during his electric fusion explorations, talks about written music being a form of enslavement to a musician's ears. I muse that his argument might also poke the folks who insist that the Bible is the only legitimate access we have to God's Living Word. If the Word Incarnate can only be found on the printed page, an illiterate believer is kinda shafted.

On the seventh day, God rested. "Rested" is not the same as "quit." The seventh note is what makes a jazz chord interesting, gives that extra puzzle piece to fit in here and there, and the rest, in music, always sets up what's coming next. Why should the Creator's Master Plan be any different? God rested, and Jesus, born of a virgin just to make things more uncomfortable, invites us into His rest. Matthew 11:28, NKJV says, "Come to Me, all you who labor and are heavy laden, and I will give you rest. Take my yoke upon you and learn from me for I am gentle and humble in heart and you will find rest for your souls."

What if we were raised in a culture that noted God spoke through music and, like the poet/playwright Ntozake Shange proposes, we each required instruments to intone the Divine? What if His song over us was the measure of our significance, and catching the chords and chorus was the same as a baby eagle learning to take the talon-caught trout from its parent? Having music is clearly an advantage, in fact a definition of our culture and civilization. Having musicians in our culture has often proved to be problematic, especially for black musicians in a culture dominated by racial tension.

Miles Davis, at the height of his career, was beat up outside one of the most famous jazz clubs in New York City because he wouldn't "move along" when a beat cop told him it was his only option. Explaining that he worked at the club, that he was in fact the headliner on the marquee, brought a billy club down on his head. A crown of thorns and the hope of glory could be the liner notes for an entire catalogue of jazz music and the indigenous recordings of a triumphant culture born of the ultimate human induced indignation: Slavery.

Complacency in music, as in worship, yields a counterfeit currency. In other words it is a calibration of celebrity as being more worthy than substance and content. The packaging outweighs the gift, like the whitewashed sepulchers of Jesus's contemporaries. Paul wrote in Colossians 3:16, NIV, "Let the word of Christ dwell in you richly as you teach one another in all wisdom, singing psalms, and hymns, and spiritual songs, making music with grace in your hearts towards God."

This is a commandment, if I can use that word for emphasis, not just for musicians, but also for all of us to become musicians and shake that tambourine in the tradition of Miriam and add more cowbell to our praise.

Talent is not the all-deciding factor in producing music. Jesus' parable about talents tells us that starting with what we have will yield an increase, but ignoring even the remotest possibility of success only guarantees our failure. I've long felt my attempts to play music would at best fall into the category of enthusiastic outsider, or worse, wanna-be interloper. Even after years of woodshedding and sporadic professional lessons, the thought of me on stage, ready to play for an audience with competent musicians, was a distant second to, say, breaking the four-minute mile mark at age sixty-four without owning a pair of running shoes.

In the spirit of "you don't know what you're capable of until you've exhausted all the ways of avoiding it," I signed up to go to a summer jazz camp. Each year, The Inside:Outside Retreat for saxophonists at Wooten Woods in Tennessee gathers horn players from around the world for a week of listening and playing jazz in a natural setting. The retreat is the brainchild of The Three Bobs: Bob Reynolds, Bob Franceschini, and Bob Hemenger — all brilliant professional saxophonists and recording artists.

In the session I attended, the second one, guest instructors included Joshua Redman, Jeff Coffin, Aaron Goldberg, Steve Wilson and a few surprise drop-ins from host Victor Wooten's stable of professional contacts. I rationalized that any musical embarrassment I was sure to suffer would be worth it if I got to talk with this marvelous bevy of musicians about their relationship with the sound of the Spirit. I was pretty certain I'd be the oldest and least experienced saxophone player at the camp. I flattered myself into believing I'd be voted most improved if I could just keep my sweaty fingers from slipping off the keys.

It was as if my favorite scripture (Psalm 37:4, NIV), which reads, "Take delight in the LORD: and He will give you the desires of your heart," was giving me yet another call to fulfill a destiny. I harbored a hope of becoming a reasonably tactful musician, despite my habitual doubts that my desires in anyway pleased the Lord. I appreciate and honor the work master saxophonists have already put in. I suspected that if God was pleased with the maestros I admired, He might, by extension, have a happy-to-help attitude toward my musical development.

Slowly, through the company of other players and believers I came to believe, as we say in our 12-step meetings, that the yearning I had to play my horn well was a foundation of my own worshipping sensibility. What could be truer than the perfect note echoing in reverential awe from a raised horn on earth projecting a new song into the very courts of the Lord's praise? Jazz aficionados would certainly attribute the integrity, purity, and power of John Coltrane's music as a bridge from the natural to the supernatural.

I had some experience playing worship sets as a volunteer minister at Pelican Bay Maximum Security Prison, but to be honest, I think the splendid acoustics of the cement block chapel reflecting the sound gave my sound its vestige of respectability. One experience at camp re-enforced the notion that I was on the right track. A fellow alto player was encouraged to find the scat singing notes he had just discovered as part of his musical DNA, on his horn, to find a voice for the music that was already in him.

To me, and everybody else in the room—whether they knew the Bible or not—it was a clear manifestation of the desires of one man's heart receiving center stage. The room of players cheering this new sound breaking through recognized the process of drawing out a God-given talent. If they are anything like me, they would mark the occasion as finding a stepping stone to cross a personal Jordan river. Scripture says God inhabits the praise of His people, and there was much to inhabit in elevating his spontaneous song of songs.

The reward of music is not only in proficiently capturing an established sound, or parroting notes off a page, but in unlocking the grace notes that save us from a wretched life of hollow gestures and tinned tunes. Somehow we have relegated the profound and personal knowledge of God to the territory of mystics, martyrs, and missionaries. It is my premise that musicians hold a key, twelve of them in fact, to unlocking the floodgates capable of redeeming the secular and the sacred, restoring the trivial to triumphant status and releasing inspired heart throbbing head banging chart toppers.

We all know we're after something, and not just because we sense somebody is ahead of us in line. The next note, the downbeat after a long pause, could be the beginning of our dance of dreams if we just get it on the good foot. The notion that we should whistle while we work is a cousin to the concept that we were made to worship. Our role in the orchestration of the universal language is a dialogue of discovery. The speak-brother-speak of jazz liturgy stems from listening to another one listening to the source of contemplation.

We aspire. Aspiration, another spirit-stemmed word breathed like the beginning of life blown into lumps of clay. I'm not one of those people who maintain the days it took to form the world were twenty-four hour periods. I don't believe the miraculous is reduced any if the separation of land and sea and the population of the skies took millenniums. Being made from dust sounds a lot like attaching one amoeba at a time to a DNA string, and like King David, it's all too wonderful for me. If there is a big playback screen awaiting us in eternity, I'll park myself down with plenty of popcorn to watch the dichotomy between Spirit and science dissolve.

Folks who doubt God's hand like to point out the pains of life and ask how God could allow such and such travesty to exist. One theory is that when we get to meet Him, He asks us the very same question—since most of life's trouble stems from the choices we make regarding our fellow planetary travelers. One choice our kind likes to make is singing with each other and it begs the question ; do we make music despite tragedy, or as an antidote?

Romans 8:26 explains that the Holy Ghost intercedes for us with groaning that cannot be uttered. For our part, we need music, sweet, sweet music. Music of the ghetto, the barrio, the cellblock, the cathedral, and maybe even the elevator and the shopping mall. The word is that the Second Coming of Christ will get our attention with a trumpet blast. As a saxophonist, I aim to be ready to echo the refrain.

We are accustomed to thinking of trajectory as a one-way street. Something in flight takes aim, and if the focus on the target is off by even a fraction, the intended contact is left gaping at the void. Worship music is sometimes portrayed as such an arrow pointing at God, hoping to hit the mark and release joyous blessings, like throwing baseballs at a clown in a dunk tank at the county fair. But if the truth is that He is pursuing us, as Jesus claims to have come seeking the lost, then maybe our songs are more like magnetic fields of reverent reverberation matching a pulsing source at the heart of the matter, the heart of a loving Father.

If we drift into worshipping music as a subtly distorted option to using music to worship, we create an idol, not an ideal. Great players often create jaw-dropping awe in an audience. Humble artists know in their souls not to take credit for the sparkling point of the performance. Realizing a God-given talent is a never-ending gift fuels them to keep studying, keep collaborating, keep practicing, and to keep progressing toward what is just out of reach, like

Michelangelo's Adam finger tipping God's outstretched palm.

There are thresholds in building faith, just as there are in building confidence, with playing an instrument. Getting an operational handle on the various fingerings and *embouchure* requirements is perhaps comparable to realizing the "Our" in the "Our Father" means we are meant to share something, or is it Someone, special with each other. As an example, the aural reality of sounding an overtone on the saxophone gives a very real experience with setting your mind on things above.

Accomplished players can multiply the range of tones hidden within a particular pitch by adjusting the air flow, but a person must hear the note before it is sounded to make the internal changes necessary to reach it consistently. I can manage four overtones on the lowest notes of my horn, but only two on most of the others. Alastar Ingram, an instructor I've reconnected with after a twenty-year hiatus, insists I learn to use a tuner to match my ordinary pitches to acceptable scales if I ever hope to develop in the altissimo range.

John Coltrane, a premier saint of the saxophone, achieved handfuls of harmonics and microtones that weren't even considered possible, let alone desirable, and forever changed the approach and attitude toward the saxophone of every player to come after him. He considered the purpose of his influence in the world of music, and of the world in general, to be spiritual, to be a force for good.

He, too, could only play what he heard, and he credited every sound, every vibration to be an emanating interpersonal gift of the Creator. He called that Creator God because, well he knew Who he was hearing from and harbored a gnawing, forever-growing sense of the unlimited tonal range of He who made the ear. The force, the gracefulness, the power, stamina and balladic presence of Coltrane's sound charges the air of the listener and underscores the sonic booming advice to keep your eye on God.

CHAPTER THREE

The Sax Camp Interviews

♪♪♪

In my writing and musical studies, I want to explore that notion of live encounters with a living God. My experiences wouldn't be enough to fill more than a few pages with notes, and the notes I play would be even less likely to command more than a few minutes attention, so I began to ask fellow musicians for their perspective. Not being a professional interviewer, I had a very short list of questions. Actually, just the one, "Did you ever bump into God when you were playing?"

I hoped something short and simple would stimulate some discussion, some discovery, and possibly, some discernment. Russ Paladino, a brilliant saxophonist and music producer living on Staten

Island was willing to sit down with me at the Inside:Outside Retreat for saxophonists and discuss his take on the matter.

(All the following interviews are reprinted with the permission of the participants.)

♫ ♫ ♫

RP: The word "God" doesn't get used a whole lot in the circles I frequent. Higher power, higher consciousness, the Spirit, are more likely terms for the source of presence, for being connected to a higher nature.

You've always had singers come out of the churches—Aretha Franklin, Whitney Houston, Luther Van Dross. The experience of music in praise of God touches people, and that influence carries on into whatever musical situations in which you find yourself.

There's something intangible about making music, especially jazz music, that puts us in a place in our minds where we are inter-connected. You could call that God, or higher consciousness, or whatever. The people I enjoy playing with share this where there is no separation between so-called secular or sacred music. It doesn't happen every time; sometimes you're just going about your business as a professional. I've absolutely had experiences where if I'm listening to myself on a recording—or even while I'm playing—that make me believe the music plays us. Since I've been meditating—I don't know if you could call it praying—I've been able to get more into that space, the present moment, where the rest of the world isn't the source of that sound I'm after. It's more of an inner ear connection.

In a workshop that morning at the camp, Steve Wilson mentioned listening to Maceo Parker, of James Brown fame whose playing always touched his heart as if he had taken a non-violent punch to the chest. I asked Russ if this ability to touch people musically was more than just a level of proficiency.

RP: Yes, many proficient musicians don't move me because they can't get past the skill that fuels their ego.

I'll tell you a story about how I met Bob Franceschini; it was too classic a coincidence to be just a coincidence. It basically changed my life. You can assign any kind of significance to it that you want. I'd been working with Latin jazz players, producing music, writing and arranging for Mongo Santamaria and Tito Puente, anybody you could imagine, and Marty Sheller wanted to produce a CD under his own name after decades of writing and arranging for other well-established musicians. There was a whole range of calamities with the recording and it was brought to me to try and fix it.

I listened to the music. It was the first time I heard Bob's playing, and I was like pinned to the wall when I heard it. I thought, Who is this guy? I have to know! *I had heard the name, but like most people I didn't know very much about him because he's not out there marketing himself. I told the guy who brought me the project I would fix it at my cost because I wanted the story to have a happy ending, but I also wanted to know if this guy, Franceschini gave lessons or whatever.*

It turned out that Bob had been living in Brooklyn but was moving to Staten Island. That seemed shocking to me because no jazz musician would ever move to Staten Island. I asked if he knew where on Staten Island he was moving, and it happened to be a five-minute walk from my house. I reached out to him and found him to be the nicest guy—very humble, very approachable.

To make a long story long, the lady Bob was with at the time, now his wife, was somebody I knew. We had played in the same circuit years ago, and since then Bob and I have become best friends. But the thing that makes it a little bit magical is at that point in time, I had not been playing music for about six years. I was just starting to get back into it, and I wanted to be playing with good guys again. I didn't really have a community of jazz friends, of guys that were sax players, and the fact that he was plopped into my life at that exact time was the exact thing that I needed in terms of friendship, camaraderie, mentoring—and if that's Divine intervention, I'd put it down as a concrete example of it in my life.

I asked Russ if the venue dictated the sacredness of the music. It would be unusual to open a set at a nightclub with, "Amazing Grace," but couldn't the event still prove to be graceful and amazing?

RP: I'm in that bubble frequently, I don't play in churches per se, but I play at a lot of wedding ceremonies, which are religious affairs more likely than not. I play for all different faiths and all sorts of religious music, and often at the same space I'll play jazz at the cocktail hour and all kinds of music at the reception. I always try to play in the headspace of being present and being connected. There is a palpable moving feeling of family that affects you as a musician. I've never thought about whether or not that makes the music better, but I've been part of some really beautiful moments—maybe at a beach or a majestic cathedral—and that exhibition of love carries into the music, and in turn, the music can carry it back to the people.

My own spiritual perspective is in a period of change. I don't talk about it much, but I grew up as a Catholic. My family wasn't particularly devout, I went to church because I walked my grandmother to Mass, and I wanted to please her and look out for her. When I hit college, I basically was like every other college kid—somewhat cynical, not particularly dialed in to anything. When I got married and had kids we had them baptized because that's the thing you did, but the experience that turned things around for me was the passing of my sister-in-law at age thirty-one and her leaving behind her children.

That was one of the reasons I stopped playing music for a while, as we had more children to look after. But the community of her church was so loving and giving and selfless. People showed up at our door with clothes or a check. I didn't even know their names, but they really helped us through that time. I felt that even if I didn't like the dogma or the structure of the church, something about the community spirit that was created was beautiful and good and godly. It seems to me that there really are forces of good and evil in this world, and if I'm going to choose which side to be on, I'm going to go that way.

These days I'm not as connected to the Catholic Church for a lot of reasons, which is why I speak in broader terms. But I absolutely believe there is something else, something bigger that I can ever hope to understand.

Last night after I came back from an airport run, as I was walking up the steps to my cabin, I looked up into the sky at all the stars. With this being a rural area, the night is black, and I happened to think how could this universe be just a random accident?

We are so infinitesimally small, and yet we're here as thinking, feeling, conscious beings. I've learned that the something that allows us to be here wants us to be respectful of love as a force for good. I'm not so comfortable yet calling that God or giving it a name. But I know it is valuable and operates in community.

I thanked Russ for his time and sensed that I was walking away with more than just notes in my workbook. The connection I felt with Russ was deeper than twenty minutes of conversation should have fostered. It was if we were both rods on a tuning fork being struck by a very soft and soothing lightning. The path we crossed was expanding into a trail, blazing of its own accord with wild berries of joy and solace ripe for the picking.

I discovered interviewing musicians was channeling me into a focus that may prove to be the theme song of my life. I couldn't wait for my next chance to sit and chat with a world-class player and discuss the other world.

♪♪♪

Mario Scaramuzza is a wonderful saxophonist and highly sought saxophone repairman from Argentina. He currently lives, studies, and works in New York City. We met outside his temporary repair workshop at the Inside:Outside Retreat for saxophonists in August of 2016, and I asked him about the possible connections of playing "in the pocket" and "in the Spirit."

>   MS: *"Playing in the pocket" is a North American term, coming from swing music, funk, anything where the groove is really the thing. We do have that too, in Argentina, but I don't know if we have a name for it, for the technical aspect.*
>
>   *For the Spirit part of it, where I come from, we have the tango, and I think there is a little more appreciation for the magical part of it. It's not as simple as do you play well, or do you not, but also, the nature of the music is more romantic, so the mood is more about the dance of love, so even the Samba, when it is well played, carries the attraction of two people. Those rhythms are*

very well known and people expect the musicians to deliver.

There are masters who play this very simply, but still surpass expectations to approach an ideal. It's sort of like a mix of the Caribbean merengue *and the Italian* parantentela *because Argentina had a big Italian immigration. So, especially in my city, there was this girl, she was playing music for her dad at night. She was studying music, classical Italian, and she came up with the bass line and added her right hand to it and it was at first kind of weird, but so many people were drawn to it.*

This style is still being played in clubs and people respond to it almost like in the '50s in the States when people were being affected by James Brown. In my town Cordoba we have this guy Carlos "La Mona" Jimenez, who's playing for thousands of people at a time, three or four nights a week for the past thirty-five years. We're talking over a hundred thousand people a month coming to hear and to dance to this music.

It's very simple, there's not a lot of flashing lights, it's just the music. It can be a nightmare gig because you play such long hours at this explosive level of energy. It is also such an expression against discrimination, because even today it is not a music of the rich. So what is shared is not just a sense of making very good music, but of making the best of life.

If you cannot play, then you cannot play. But if you have certain abilities, you can let go and just let sound be there, to be of service. Music is a powerful source of growth. There are people who can take music and make you feel like you, yourself, can do amazing things.

Some people are notorious for this. I choose music for my life because I am a little bit out, I want to think there is something cosmic about it. If you grow up eating canned vegetables you will never know what something fresh tastes like. Music is the same way. If not, I would have sold shoes or something because it is a lot easier way to make money.

Playing music for a living is an ever-expanding education. And musicians are getting smarter about behavior, about making choices, about broadening their horizons by sampling other cultures. It's a great job to make you start thinking.

The levels of complexities that our society offers us are constantly dumbing down. In the fifties and sixties the comprehension of language needed to read a newspaper was equivalent to an eighth grade education, now it's down to about fifth or maybe sixth. We are letting people take away from our culture what is precious. Who takes the time anymore to contemplate the greenery all around us as something beautiful, as something intrinsic to a human being to be able to appreciate and recognize life for what it is?

Jazz is one of the elements that builds this awareness and tries to establish a culture of listening. Some great shit is out there in the world of pop music, of hip-hop, but it's like the same meal for everybody, every time they sit down to a meal. It seems like celebrity status replaced substance. Myself being a foreigner—I'm from Argentina and married to an African American—I get to see how popular American culture is around the world because of the contribution of black culture. With people around the world, America is great because of James Brown, Louis Armstrong, Duke Ellington, Michael Jackson, and, well, Michael Jordan too.

Black music is just so freaking cool. You have all the problematics of race in America, but outside of America, it's the music that represents. It's completely overlooked here in the states because it is politically charged, and it is hard to talk about. People wish that what happens to black people in this country was a closed discussion, that it has been resolved, but it hasn't. It's an on-going theme, something that we each have to learn how to live with. When I see teenagers in the building where I live doing things that if I respond, as a Caucasian, will get them into deep, deep trouble, I have to stop and think myself out of the immediate dogma that says this is right and this is wrong.

You have to develop good ears so you can hear the help that is available to the situation. That is the mission. The way we feel inside comes through. If you put a beautiful message out, it will get to people somehow. Some people know this, and some people just move along like cattle.

It takes a lot of work just to get out of the bed that is in your head. Music is a great tool for that, man. t is a great teacher. We are told that we are so basic, that we can only understand a picture in front of us, or some gathering of words. But we are built to get and give more than that. Learning to play an instrument with other people can teach you a lot about life, and how to improve it.

In our constant attempt to dominate what is beyond our control we have created, for example, a tuning system that is not 100 percent natural. Sometimes what it takes is just to bang on the piano like a kid. It is true that if you don't know the song, you're going to suck. You're not going to touch anybody. If you're out of tune, it doesn't matter how much spirit you put into it. That's the work of aesthetics—you have to put that in, you have to learn the rules you're playing with, so you can go just outside of them into vibration, into the truth of it.

We make music this thing, but music is a lot of things that are not just the things it is made up of. We are here to learn, and a lot of people are taught that they are too old to learn anything new.

I didn't really have a plan, but I have to step aside and see that the people, the musicians I admired and respected are the people I am now breaking bread with. They are the people who are hiring me to do work.

When you think about it, what are the chances that an architectural student from Argentina would get a scholarship into one of the highest level music schools in the States? I had just met this beautiful American girl who was to become my wife and we were in the apartment. We had this cassette. All the musicians in the city, we passed on all the music we could get our hands on, to each other. This cassette featured Bob Franceschini who was like 27 at the time, playing with Marty Sheller. He was burning, playing this hot Latin music and that was the sound, that was the tenor that I got to hear.

I was going to architectural school, and I was also playing music and fixing horns. That was my love, and my wife, who is very savvy as every woman is, was thinking, "How do I get this dude to go to the States?" because she, too, wanted to go to school.

My all-time dream since I was sixteen, seventeen, was to go to NY and study music. She presents it to me like this, "We could go to NY for a year or two. I'll finish my masters, and you can study with these cats you are listening to. Then we can come back, and you can do your thing."

How can you say no to that? A beautiful woman telling you to live out your dream?

We did it, man. We just went for it, and when I was bringing in all my papers to school, I was wondering, "Where will I be in the American system?" I did the audition and got into music school. Actually, I applied for both—for architectural school as well. The music school gave me a scholarship, and all of a sudden it's like, "Wow you start next semester."

So now every time I want to jump off a bridge I have to stop and think about this, how it came to be. I mean I did put a little muscle into it, but how this came together, it is a lot. It is too much to just be a casual thing.

Right now I feel like I'm in the middle of the storm, but I found a new faith. There is a bigger picture than me accomplishing, or not accomplishing, my dreams, *or having the approval of others, or not. I am trying, through music, to give up even my own approval. I want to play certain things, for a whole year it f#*+%^%g sucks. Perhaps it does, but it doesn't belong to me. It is not mine to judge. I don't only belong only to myself. Ego can only destroy the ability to learn about love. Learning to be honest. If you're not Charlie Parker, you're not Charlie Parker, but you are an amazing creature making sounds with a piece of metal that someone invented 200 years ago. There is something else that is powerful playing through you. It helps you if you stay in tune with other people and don't get it the way.*

In a way it's like a priesthood. People give up so much to play music; financial security, family time, lots of ordinary things. I was talking to a kid the other day—he eats ramen noodles every day, but he has a three thousand dollar saxophone. He has found his mission. Many times we don't realize the levels of luxury we have in this life. But music isn't just a luxury. It's not just something to have in the background; it is a foundation of peace. It is a way to live correctly, to be useful, to be generous, to be contemplative.

♫ ♫ ♫

A tradition at the Inside:Outside Retreat is to have a player—maybe a guest artist or a staff member—play the camp into mealtime with a reverential improvisation. The concept was at first introduced as being "in lieu" of prayer, because even the word "prayer" can apparently set some people off in a wrong direction.

I requested that the spokesman drop what I felt to be an over-correction since I, at least, was not disturbed by prayer as a descriptive term. My point was accepted and the pre-meal music was allowed to become more of a meditation of the harmonies of humanism and a higher power.

The great promise of the spirit of improvisational music is that preparation can lead to the discovery of what the music needs from moment to moment. The great paradox of the same spirit is when the depth of the musical moment is recognized, the music seems to play itself. The harmony of the musicians involved is maximized. The sense of hearing what the other players are hearing echoes along steep canyons and vast mountains of connection. The probability of a note rippling across each player's pond of awareness and ability approaches 80 to 90 percent of compatible comprehension, even, at times, surpassing 100 percent.

Something happens. A faith-based culture might say Somebody happens. A body of substance, not mere celebrity, begins to sing a new song. The sphere of expectation musicians enter while improvising is a sincere foundation for excitement, exploration, even exhortation. There is something to work with because of inspiration, there is inspiration because of the work put in. Bob Reynolds, saxophonist, composer, recording artist, and the internet's most generous instructor, calls it listening to the music that's not yet there.

Bob says it's the musician, not just the instrument, that's the vessel. The goose bumps come from producing the sounds that include a stillness dedicated to executing whatever comes into the attentive opportunity. He tells a story, and backs it up with a recording of the event, when the music produced on the bandstand was way more than the sums of its parts, as if, "a fifth person joined in" through some portal of projected intent. The simple suggestion that the bass player, Janek Gwizdala, "just do something" led to a spiraling loop of intricate intimacy that electrified the integral intensity of the group's performance.

♪ ♪ ♪

I didn't interview the camp's guest artist, Joshua Redman, but gleaned a few things from a talk he gave at a breakout session. I did manage to get a smile from him, which isn't all that difficult, when I said I had heard his father, Dewey Redman, play a dozen times or so in the 1970s. The person responsible for giving me my first saxophone, a Cleveland high school level tenor, came with me to hear Dewey once and remarked the elder Redman was the most obnoxious saxophonist he'd ever heard. The anecdote caught Joshua a bit by surprise, as you might expect, but got a guffaw of recognition and permission to highlight a few points from Joshua's talk to an assembled room of fifty or so saxophonists.

Joshua's first point, after explaining that he doesn't speak well in public, or private either, when he stopped to think about it, is that players today have so much access to everything possible there is to learn or hear in the world of jazz that it is important to guard against homogenization of the standards.

"Jazz is at its best," he said, "when it's highly subjective, personal, quirky, and very close to being just wrong. That's being in the moment with room to realize the moment is why we came here."

"It's hard for me to remember how I approached certain things, or how I solved locating myself in situations where I didn't have all the pieces to the puzzle. I've been around musicians my whole life that are freaks of nature. They have perfect pitch, they can remember any song after only hearing it once, or twice. Those things are rare, but they're not that rare when you get to the upper echelon of players. I am not one of those, I gravitated toward music I loved, and found the more I did that, the more I loved it.

"What I responded to, almost from the get go, were the feelings, the emotions music created in me, or in a room full of people. I mean playing clean lines over chord changes is legitimate, but what I was going for in the beginning of my playing was that physically receptive lick that seemed like it could change your heart rate.

"There is a difference between a live audience and an audience that's alive. Before I knew what jazz was, I knew it was a participatory event, with people in a room, before it was something that came over the radio or from a recording. That thing, whatever you call it—emotion, soul, groove—is what musician aspire to bring into being. You can't fake that. It is either really there or really missing. There is this something that is super conscious, universal, and funky all at the same time. It's serious fun to experience playing with people that can combine love and joy.

"The engine of self criticism can only run around in your mind, in your life, if it has fuel, and for years that was my reaction every time I stopped playing and started to think about what I played. I couldn't put the horn down without immediately kicking my own ass for what I played, or didn't play. Some of that was a desire to get better, for the most part those of us who play music for a living have a degree of that. There are a few players who think they are the shit, and really are—that's getting back to those freaks of nature—but most of us wonder how we got as far as we are, and how are we connecting to what's next.

"I still feel like playing a decent blues is the hardest thing, probably because I value it so much. I have some ideas, and I have some experience, but when I hear a master, I'm just decimated every time. Maybe it's because the way musicians lived in previous generations came out of such a difficult life. Today's jazz is more of a world music, but the roots came from black people living in America during those times in history when that wasn't ideal."

♫ ♫ ♫

The Inside:Outside Retreat for saxophonists is housed at Victor Wooten's Nature camp outside of Only, Tennessee. It is also home to the Wooten clan, so we campers had the bonus of hearing Drummer Roy "Futureman" Wooten's lecture on the book, *New World Symphonies: How American Culture Changed European Music* by Jack Sullivan.

In an opening chapter about new world rhythms being bred of jazz, the cultural history of musical exchange between Europe and America, especially black America, is noted for a period of nearly 100 years where the improvisational differences between classical European music and American jazz were blurred. European composers began to consider American jazz composures as the real classical American musical voice. It was understood at the time that European composers were indifferent to American symphony writers but were entranced by the original and vibrant works coming from such genius composers as Jelly Roll Morton, Art Tatum, and Duke Ellington.

In this country, jazz was relegated to a subculture, really a low-life status of whorehouse music. For jazz to develop into something that would take over the whole world was really something unexpected. The champions for this music were the reigning European composers of the day. Dvorak, one of the most celebrated composers in history, was specifically brought to America to assist the new world in developing its own culturally based art music. He was particularly taken by the Negro spiritual music which he said, "Answered Wagner at every turn." He instructed his students to sing "Go

Down Moses" on the same concert stage previously devoted to Bach and Beethoven.

Debussy, Stravinsky, Ravel, and their contemporaries drank in the rhythms of jazz as if it were an elegant elixir of egalitarianism. Even the sudden use of saxophones in boleros speaks to the pouring in of the jazz voice to the European sound. The first jazz opera, "Jonny Spielt Auf," composed by Ernst Krenek in 1925, celebrated the triumph of the new world over the old, crediting jazz with striking the emblematic notes of the times. The roar of the Twenties crossed the Atlantic on the rhythms of jazz. The highly personal jazz epiphanies experienced by European composers compelled them to express the exaltations first echoed in the field hollers and church choruses of Black American culture.

Jazz is still a young music. Charlie Parker said jazz was writing short stories, but would soon convert to writing novels. The accepted length of European compositions gave weight to the stories it told. Incorporating the new sounds into traditional forms was a tactical experiment designed to give room for jazz compositions to take their place in the canon of world-class storytelling. The new music was seeping through the cracks of the old world order, paving the way for a new reality.

When Rachmaninoff came to America, the first place he went was to Harlem, to hear Art Tatum. The maestro told Tatum he may eventually be able to match him in speed but could never hope to equal the improvisational skill the jazzman used night after night. Rachmaninoff said that if Tatum ever turned his talents towards European concert music all the European greats would be in trouble to salvage their reputations.

In another celebrated example Roy Wooten related, Vladimir Horowitz, who has been studying Tatum's "Tea for Two," was very pleased for an opportunity to play it for him over the phone. As a gift, Tatum played a new arrangement back for him. When Horowitz asked for the sheet music for the new version so he could study it, Tatum told him there wasn't any as he had just made it up on the spot. The love affair between these great art forms of European traditionally composed classical music and American spontaneously composed jazz music shares a history of cultural exchange that bodes well for future contributions of either style. Art music allows the whole world to hear itself reflected back and projected forward at the same time. The expression of our souls, the sound of Spirit is the sudden rush of joy escaping the confines of anguish. And music, the language we all deem as universal, comes closest to that when it bridges genres, generations, and generalizations.

♫ ♫ ♫

Hernan Sosa is a saxophonist from Peru. He works in a copper mine for his day job outside of Lima, driving a few miles up the mountain and descending almost the same distance inside the mountain to get at the ore. We had a few moments at the airport in Nashville after the Inside:Outside Retreat to talk and I asked him how music helped him to make sense of the world.

> *HS: When I play, back in Peru, I feel every time that I am kind of connecting the people listening to something larger than us, but something that we have in common, even though it is way beyond what we can see. Music allows every person to hear that they have a*

spiritual potential to be connected. It is there to be discovered, to be worked out. Music is often connected to ceremony. Even before the Spanish came to Peru, the Incas used music to celebrate their way of life. I have friends now who say they can't believe in an invisible God, but when they hear or play music, they know something alive is living in them. I play a saxophone, but if I don't blow into it, nothing comes out. Our life is like that—something has to blow life into us.

Energy is all around us—plants, people, animals—we are all vibrating. People are comfortable to know something about that, but maybe not too much, because it is something individual, and something we share. It is easier to marvel at creation than to consider there is a Creator.

Tradition and culture begin to define who we are, but we have more and more opportunity to connect with other people. Music, especially jazz music, contributes to that. Every culture has its base. We have Afro-Peruvian music, and when you hear it, even at a restaurant, everyone wants to dance to this, even my mother. We too, like America, had a slave culture brought over by the Spanish.

I am a mixed race, maybe that's why I like jazz because of some roots in my blood. There is no obligation to listen or appreciate this kind of music. It is not even on the radio; we only have pop music. But each generation has been passing this music on, and adding something to it, for four hundred years.

We have a really good trumpet player from Peru; he is now playing in New York. Gabriel Alegira. He is bringing this music from an outlaying area back to the jazz center of the world and making it new again. He is inspiring all of us, people in Peru, people in New York. He is teaching at NYU. You could say he has moved mountains because he has helped two very different cultures become closer together—now I am coming to a music camp in Nashville, USA, to play with an American bass player, Ross Kratter who played with Gabriel.. So you see the very large world is coming together on the same stage, for the same reason—the love of music.

♫ ♫ ♫

Thieme Schipper is a recording artist from the Netherlands. He plays saxophone and flute, composes original music, and has been known to arrange traditional Christian hymns into contemporary jazz voicings. We shared a cabin at the Inside:Outside Retreat with saxophonists from six continents and seventeen countries. One other thing we shared was an admiration for Kirk Whalum's playing.

One of Thieme's instructors tried to shy him away from using a tune by Whalum on his debut recording, as the instructor felt a Christian theme just wasn't somehow pure enough to put on a jazz album. Thieme stuck to his initial plan. The quality of Kirk Whalum's playing and writing is at such a high level of artistry as to render any out-of-hand dismissal as musically absurd.

> *TS: "I come across that a lot—that resistance to combine emotionality with spirituality. But when something hits you so hard as being something special, something unexpected, it challenges your awareness. It makes distinguishing between emotion and spirit difficult."*

Kirk Whalum tells a story on his recording, *The Gospel According to Jazz Part 2*, of having difficulty writing an arrangement when a sudden, almost toss-off musical phrase, came to him in a studio session, which he knew was from God who also, almost incidentally, told him who to record it with, Jonathon

Butler the great guitarist from South Africa. Was the phrase better than anything he would of come up with on his own? The outside listener may have trouble verifying any distinction. A burning bush is not thought to be an everyday sort of experience, getting a note, or a chord, to fit, just so, in a musical composition may not seem to be on equally miraculous footing, but there are turns of a musical phrase that have turned the ears of the entire world.

♫ ♫ ♫

I wrote a poem to spell out the Speller

God is the only One Who's heard it all before,
every whisper tone tenor in every juke joint joining
 the jumble
of julep glasses and payday smiles, every under-the-
 breath grunt
of the pine-top piano player counting his honey keys
 and the vocalisms
of the fronting singer whose voice may have been
 golden or silver in youth
but has bronzed and brassed with the crowd's
 applause or indifference.

"Why's the devil got all the good music?" is the
 revivalist organist's
accelerando.
"Well, he don't," is what God says from a back
 corner booth,
everything that has breath hanging on His every
 word.

Rackety crickets pop outside the window, crispy
 flying things
Fry in the zapper blowing killer stanzas under the
 porch awning.
Willow leaves whisper in their own night, nightingales
 prove
the point in their black eyes is a star from a cymbal
 ride
that has even the lamest feet tapping.

You want glory realized?
Trace the walking bass to the blindless place

and the all-seeing grace of the swirling skirts raising
  the dust
we are made of into a cloud of praise.

CHAPTER FOUR

Praise Raises More Than an Eyebrow

♪♪♪

Steve Clark operates in worshipful overflow. As a singer, guitarist, and bandleader at Lifehouse Church in Humboldt County, California, he encourages people to experiment, to experience their own tone in a collaborative ringing of the spiritual bell of gratitude and enthusiasm. The Good Book counsels us to "Rejoice in the Lord, always" (Philippians 4:4, NIV). For Steve it pares down to a mantra of, "Calm Fears, Raise Hopes." His music incorporates a willingness to express what his heart hears, with a commitment to listen for others' hearts. To facilitate such listening, the worship team plays in the round, facing each other in a circle surrounded by the congregation. The separation factor of being a band on stage facing a passive audience is set aside in favor of a group gathering steam together to rise as one voice.

The physical roundhouse floor plan at the Arcata Lifehouse campus came from brainstorming with Pastor Willy Bowles to make an intimate temple environment, as an alternative to traditional seating arrangements. The light in the room comes from the center, much like a campfire, and the privacy of the shadows allows the worshippers to dance, to shout, or to snore in safety.

This is where I first heard Steve and the band play, and where I've chosen to land as a congregant ever since. Steve explained that the circular sound concept presents technical issues of feedback and distortion that still challenge the musicians and sound crew.

> *SC 'It's dicey, the speakers are directly above us, so getting centered for microphones and amplifiers and all that is always an issue. That being said, the payoff is amazing. It's the best place I've ever played to do worship within a community. I've played on bigger stages with tons of people in the room, but it still doesn't hold a candle to everybody being packed in, and in it together. It's very hard to lead a group of people respectfully when*

they're staring at you and you're staring back at them. The extra bit of inclusion you get is with the band because you're all in the circle looking at each other.

"In the rock music setting, the leader is walking all over the stage, interacting with the crowd and the band. It's hard not to be the focal point. But in the circle, it's a whole different thing, you can egg each other on with just a smile. It's really cool. We've been doing it for about three years now, and we're beginning to see videos of others places picking up on the idea. But it's mostly stripped down to an acoustic folk style, not the full-on rock band feel. I'm not seeing anybody doing it for church, but I haven't been looking for it either."

Steve is a tall, lanky man slinging a six-string hollow body guitar. I asked him how it came about that occasionally he breaks into a falsetto voice that might seem more fitting in the Viennese Boy's Choir.

SC: "It's come from the harmonies I heard growing up—The Beach Boys, The Commodores Heroes *album, Larry Norman. All those guys tended to match their vocals to the emotion they wanted to project. That always moved me. It was highlighted in my spirit. It takes you somewhere that the normal belting it out can't take you. The vulnerable feeling behind it has always grabbed me. However, even if it feels natural for me to go there, I'm trying to lead a congregation in a song. I know they won't be able to match the notes, but the moment of the emotional spiritual connection that voicing allows is worth the risk."*

Steve continued to explain the organization required to allow the worship band members to worship as individuals. "The structure of a song is very important, but the question becomes 'Can we give more than just that structure, or can we begin to approximate what God wants to get back from giving us the song in the first place?'

SC: "We develop a trust among ourselves for the talent, and the anointing, that brings us together into the music. There are times in worship when I'll know something is there, I'll sense something needs to happen to release like a knockout punch, and I'll literally call out into the microphone for it to happen. Because we play to relate to each other, in a context of relating to Spirit, we can implement the give and take in a way we couldn't if it was just random people rotating through a song cycle. You don't want train wrecks, and mutual appreciation of ability is part of that protection.

"The mindset that controls most Christian church music is that you, as a leader, don't want to lose the

congregation by going off into these areas. I get that, but I don't see how you can lose anyone if the Holy Spirit is the song leader and the band is just following the anointing. I truly believe that the anointing on a musician can take people deeper into worship than where the musician could take them by himself.

"There is a big difference between a song leader and a worship leader. A few years ago, when I realized God was taking me down a path of becoming a worship pastor, I realized you can't be everything to everybody, you just can't. But the bridge to reach anyone, at any time, is the anointing on the moment. Not everyone likes my flavor, but when I'm operating out of the anointing, the flavor, my style, doesn't get in the way of reaching people, because everyone can grab a hold of the love of God.

"Sometimes you just have to get out of the way. Even last night, something was being released sonically that was touching people spiritually that words, lyrics, wouldn't have been able to express. You could sense the band agreeing to back off and just let that sit for a moment. There are times when we—my daughter MacKensie and I—will blend harmonies, just rising oohs *and* ahhs, *just textured, vocalized breathing to match the motion, the emotion, of the Holy Spirit being released into the room. Those intimate moments are so*

much fun. I love those moments, you're not saying anything but you're hearing everything He needs to say.

"Most of the music I grew up listening to in church was written by people I've never met, whether it is a traditional hymn, or something contemporary coming out of the '80s or '90s. I really feel that if you're going to pastor the direction of worship for a group of people, you have to know your identity. Part of your identity is your sound.

"Being comfortable in your sound comes from playing your heart out. The sound of your heart is the point you lead people from, that's the sound of Spirit coming through as genuine. The next level in worship music is the same as in so-called worldly stuff. It's the original sound that sets music apart. The Rolling Stones started out as a cover band, doing American blues tunes, but their hit, their break-through song, was their sound coming through the years of tradition that they tapped into as they were learning what they needed to sound like to be themselves.

"The flipside is U2. They did nothing but their own tunes, to their detriment. There is a story of them being asked to play a medley of Beatle tunes at a benefit show, and they couldn't do it because they only knew the chords to their own songs. I believe it is very important to

realize there is a spiritual component to being original. God created us to be original and the church, for some reason, has come up with this idea that everything has to sound the same. It's a real bummer.

"I believe God deserves the entire rainbow spectrum of sounds, from the blues artists, to rap artists, to everything in between. And I believe those sounds could be released in worship music. As pastors, that's the direction we aim to pursue. My big passion is to help people find their sound. Not everyone is called to be a soloist or a front man, but there is a Jonathon-anointing that is a supporting role, a morphing into whatever sound is trying to be achieved. That's my heart—to help people find themselves ringing inside the bell of sound we create and to release the attentive, worshipful, note they carry."

♫ ♫ ♫

When my family attends the worship service Steve leads, we sit between a church elder who enjoys the music, as it doesn't require a hearing aid, and students younger than our youngest child. The mix of folks is not just generational, but cultural, racial, economic, and political. The unifying force is the universal source of grateful hearts everywhere.

The roundhouse effect invokes an almost sweat lodge atmosphere of closing out the city's night and the country's plight. Street drunks emerge from their sleeping bag cocoons to shout, sometimes in conjunction with the music, sometimes not, as dancers fill an overlooking loft with swirls of color. Choruses rise to crescendos and fall to echoing whispers for the better part of an hour. The room tunes to the silence around the sound. What is the Spirit singing? What revelations are circulating on the wings of the dove? The effort to perceive is concerted, even in what might appear to be a concert setting. The lyrics on the mounted screens are guides to what is written on the hearts of the worshipers, and sometimes—in fact, more often than not—the music is put into a holding trance pattern to allow a community prophet to speak, or for a prayer request to be made known.

I have never been in battle. My brother is a combat veteran, as are some of my longtime friends. I sometimes wonder if this music on the frontlines of spiritual warfare would be recognizable for its strategy and intensity to such an observer.

Scripture (Ephesians 6:12, Message translation) says our battle is no afternoon athletic contest we'll forget about in a few hours. This is for keeps, a life or death fight to the finish against the devil and all his deceit. Bullets and blood on one hand, church bulletins and folks sitting smugly in their pews on the other. It may be hard to draw any correlation between the two, but all evil in the world comes by human willingness to side with selfish desires. Without human co-operation, demons, fallen angels, tyrants, and criminals are powerless.

If worship music can strike a chord toward harmony and the purposes of compassion and commonsense, then shouting from the rooftops what is revealed in secret chambers is indeed the best offense and good defense. The concept is hardly new. David, and all his mighty men, played music before God with all their might, with singing, on harps, on stringed instruments, on tambourines, on cymbals, and with trumpets. Sounds like a jam session to me.

The operational principle of praise music comes from Psalm 22:3, New Living Translation, "Yet You art holy, You Who inhabit the praises of Your people." We all appreciate signs and words of affection, and if the living God is that, i.e. living and God, then the reality of communication, with holy communion, should follow the same courtesies of conversation we employ with our loved ones. Sincerity, not flattery; connection, not affectation; and honest response rather than guarded calculation.

The confirmation of being heard is one of the most profound experiences a married couple can exchange, and we, as the bride of Christ, have the option to partake in the divinely natural as both the wooing partner, and the pursued lover, during every phase of the deifying courtship.

Sound reasoning is sometimes complimented by the phrase, "I hear that." Identifying with the speaker is often the goal of anyone addressing himself or herself to a crowd. Whether that person is a worship leader singing to a cloud of witnesses, or the Spirit crooning to a gathering of saints, the same measure of success holds true. We bop our heads, clap our hands, snap our fingers, and move our feet. The beat goes on because the beat is the most recognizable facet of the universal language we call music. I have no doubt the same applies to spiritual music.

🎵🎵🎵

It just happened to be his 29th birthday when I sat down to speak with Joel Valle, a bi-lingual multi-instrumentalist and musical coach at the Bethel School of Supernatural Discipleship about the role of drums and percussion in worship music. Joel nodded, as if setting a tempo, before replying.

JV: "Drums, a lot goes into it. Rhythm comes before notes, before scales. I assume that when the Pilgrims got here, drums were—for lack of a better word—kind of a savage thing. In other cultures— Middle Eastern, African, Native Americans—drums have been used in worship for centuries.

"America is still a young country, and aside from military parade music, I don't think drums had been brought into the culture until the last few decades. For me it's a combination of social science, community building, and mathematics. Counting out a 4/4 beat or a 6/8 or whatever, creates a basis. Spiritually, drums are the sound of breakthrough, of shaking the room. It's a sound of warfare, of letting go. When I lay down a syncopated sort of Latin thing, I'm hoping people are moved to jump,

to dance, so that even if they don't jump or dance, they know there's permission.

"It can be a little uncomfortable, because most of the people in that room, the Sunday night service, are Caucasian, they're white. I grew up listening to Santana music and, worship wise, to the sounds coming out of the Vineyard movement in the late '90s—a lot of jump to jump sound, heavy syncopated toms, djembe. That's what really got me into the very charismatic doomp-pah-dheemp *kind of feel. It's in my blood and my culture.*

"My parents are both Mexican immigrants, but our music, even our worship music at home was heavily influenced by Cuban sounds—Tito Puente on timbales. It's very natural for me for music to be fun. I carry that when I'm playing—whether it is on drums, or rhythm guitar, even vocals. That's what I like to release when I'm playing. I would like everyone to buy into that, but there's a little bit of tension. Some people were brought up in very religious types of homes, and any kind of jungle music is relegated to the stuff of demons and witchcraft. But God is bigger than that. The Lord is redeeming the beat. It's just going to take a while.

"The Lord's been talking to me lately, and it's weird—well that's always weird, but it's a good weird. I'm going to say that I'm a naturally talented musician,

but I'm not that skilled. I don't read music very well. I'm not very disciplined. I've never taken a drum lesson or watched a YouTube video on drumming—just a lot of listening and jamming with buddies.

"There are one or two students here who are incredibly classically trained, and it's uncomfortable having people I'm supposed to coach who are better musicians than I am. But as I said, the Lord's been talking to me and emphasizing that before I was a musician, I was a worshiper. I was trying to sing when I was four years old. I just wanted to make a sound that would burst out with everything that was going on inside of me. The reason I'm not a cookie cutter, KLOVE, copy drummer is that I don't have that studio type of discipline, I don't have a less-is-more type of background.

"I started playing drums almost by accident. I was a rhythm guitar player for a Hispanic church that used another church's facilities. We rehearsed in their space on Tuesday or Thursday, and they had a house drum set. They put away the drumsticks and everything so kids wouldn't get on the set during the week. I'd been playing guitar for about two years and piano for one. I walked up to the drum set and sat down with two pencils. I began to play a sort of boom-twa *rhythm. I had listened to enough music so that it sort of made sense, but just then*

my pastor came into the room and caught me playing. I immediately dropped the pencils and said, 'I'm sorry. It will never happen again,' because I thought I was in trouble. But he said, 'Sit down and do that again.'

"I was still fumbling around and apologizing, and he said again, 'Sit down and play that again.' So I played some kind of shuffle beat with the pencils and he said, 'That is awesome. I'm going down to the music store tomorrow to buy you some sticks and brushes. You're our new drummer.'

"I said, 'Pastor, I'm not a drummer. I play rhythm guitar.' He stopped me right there and said, 'I was a music major in college; you don't want to argue this with me. I know what I heard, and you're our new drummer.' So that's how I started at age thirteen, and I've been soaking up influence ever since. It's become my heart.

"It seems like every church has two or three guitar players and a handful of singers that want to lead worship, but no drummers. This door has been opened for me to serve a worship team, to serve a worship leader, a worship pastor. It's been kind of a rough road for me at times because I have a big personality—and coming from a small town, all I ever wanted to be was the leader, the rock star.

"I'm somewhat proficient as a musician, but now, even though I do get to lead worship and sing sometimes, I'm a better leader because I became a drummer first. As long as I'm not called on to be slick, I can lead people into having fun while worshipping. And on Sunday nights, that's what we're called on to do—to leave it all on the field and drum until my hands hurt. Not because it's a performance, but because people have jobs, they have schedules, bills to pay, they have health issues, family matters, and if for two hours on a Sunday we can encourage people, then let's do it.

"In a way the Sunday night band I play with is like a bunch of barbarians coming in from the cold. We don't play safe music. We shout, we scream, we yell. Justin Grimaldo on guitar is a major shredder. Noah Watkins on bass comes from a heavy metal, head-banging background, and he brings that. We recently added Michael Luhrs on percussion. We take it all in and yeah, I have to be civil sometimes, and leave some room. I am concentrating, about 80 percent of where I'm at is focused, supportive drumming. But part of the release, part of the reason is love. Loving what I'm doing, loving who I'm doing it with, and loving God for setting me on this path and populating it with other worshippers.

"I am more skilled than when I first began playing, but I think where I hear the Holy Spirit most is when I'm out of the way. Maybe I've just finished a swelling crescendo on the cymbals, and this orbit in the atmosphere grabs us and we begin to float, to circulate and let go of whatever we brought into the room, to let the Holy Spirit breathe into us again."

🎵🎵🎵

One of the tenets of the church Steve and Joel belong to is a cultural shift toward encounters with God in a genuine community. I asked Joel how music fits into shifting a culture.

JV: "The students I coach listen to live music five or six designated hours a week—not even counting two more hours on Sunday. It's almost too much. When you think back a few generations, access to live music was a very rare experience.

"I challenge them to search for what they want music to do for themselves. What do you want imparted to you through the music? The proof is in the pudding. Most of the students are already competent musicians, so where they need the most encouragement is in relationship. It's important to get the songs down, to get the time right, even on a simple song with only four chords, a chorus,

and a bridge. But as far as impartation, it's up to the individual to seek what supernaturally can be added to the person's natural ability.

"I had an experience in Oaxaca Mexico—in a little village, way up the mountain. After a long and nauseating drive, we were visiting a little church. It was very rural—most of the elder people there didn't even speak Spanish. They had a worship band setting up—bass, drums, keyboard. But the guitarist was called away that week. I was helping out by setting up chairs, I had no intention of playing music, although just as I was leaving home for the trip the Lord told me to take a guitar and be ready.

"The church's guitar was on the stage and somebody on our team mentioned that I was a guitar player back home. The band was less than enthusiastic about me sitting in last minute, as they were concerned I wouldn't know the music. But I was brought up on this music called Corritos, so I had my ears open. When they began this sort of cumbia beats, I walked right in and start jamming. The moment became something special for me as I mixed in sort of a bluesy riff in D. The musicians became very excited, very appreciative of my American style. I realized that everything I had been playing around with for the past ten or fifteen years had a

purpose and lead me right up to that moment, that chorus.

"I jammed with that band for two days, til my fingers were bleeding from the rusty strings. People came up to us and told us how the music inspired them and how moving it was to have the two cultures come together in the music. One young boy in the audience told us he wanted to start saving his money to go to music school in the city.

"I had another experience just a few years ago when I went with some of the students here to Cambodia. Once again, a last minute nudge, this time from my bass player, Joaquin, got me to take a guitar. I was actually looking forward to a break from music. I didn't know anything about Cambodia and told myself it was OK for me to go over there and just be some sort of sponge to their culture. We wound up playing music in every orphanage we visited, every church that hosted us, and even playing a Christian worship set on the stage of a Hard Rock Café` in this predominantly Buddhist culture.

"I may never become an international famous recording artist, but I've already been able to put love first and have it impact people in different cultures, different countries. My sound today reflects that—it's bigger, with more space for His presence."

Joel's perspective reminded me how drums work. They do their thing because a soft membrane, a skin, is stretched over a hollow echo chamber and touched by an outside source of energy and intent.

We have skin; we have echo chambers in our heart. And more than we might suspect, we are very similar to drums. The spiritually discerning among us might propose that we are also perpetually touched by an outside source of energy and intent.

Joel observed that his experience, playing the drums in worship, often leads to a spiritual breakthrough in the room and in the band. Tempo and temperament seem to march together in harmony.

A sense of the times we're in is often portrayed as an electronic quickening of stress, information overload, and polarization of the have's and have not's. Perhaps the call of the drum to something universal is the pulse and pause we need to hear to find our place in a compassionate community. "We got the beat" is hard to beat as a rallying cry. Keeping time on a high hat, or a floor tom, is not just waiting around for something to happen—it is laying the groundwork, the foundation, for something to rise up and be counted.

A drummer, using all four limbs, goes out on a limb, to make sure all the branches of a song have a root, a trunk, a body. Every piece of music has a one, a downbeat, a place to start and a place to return our innate attention. A song leader never asks the audience, or congregation, to clap along on the offbeat, even in jazz circles the pickup note is left to professionals. Reggae music plays on the upbeat to play with our heads, and create the swaying island feel even in our land-locked ghettoes, but the bottom is always in place in the face of complacency.

For lack of a better term, world music has emerged as the description of music not native to the English-speaking world, and the first recognizable facet of music from another culture is always the beat. I've heard percussionists hypothesize that if we ever do communicate with extraterrestrials it will be because playing the clave`, two beats against three in a count of four, will prove fascinating to whatever aliens use for ears. Can we also summon angels by tapping sticks and brushes? If Gabriel is any kind of section man, or soloist, he'll be alert for the rim shot that says, "Jump in anytime!"

Long ago, in a desert far, far, away it all started with Miriam, on the tambourine, praising God for parting the Red Sea. We applaud such efforts without stopping to think, "Where did this 'automatic' response of clapping our hands together come from?"

Before instruments—possibly even before song—we clapped, we tapped our feet, maybe even snapped our fingers. We mark our place with an accent beat. This is where we stand, this is where we dance, this is where we live. And if this is where we live, then so does Whomever we credit with getting us this far.

The coffee cup mantra urges us to sing as if nobody is listening, and to dance as if nobody is watching, painting a picture of an empty universe of shadows and lights. The position of faith is to have as much fun in selfless expression as possible, while entertaining the hope and promise that Someone is always listening with appreciation, affection, and affinity for our function in infinity and—need I say it?—beyond.

♪ ♪ ♪

Watching Naoko Rivera have fun behind a drum set was almost as much a surprise to me as it was for her to be there after a twenty-five-year hiatus from playing drums in a high school band in Japan. Her path back to the drum throne began during a mission trip to Australia. Her group was asked to consecrate an abandoned building with amazing acoustics.

A member of the team had brought a guitar and a hand drum but couldn't play both, so the request for a drummer prompted a friend to nominate Naoko. Coincidentally, her connection to the Spirit had been nudging her to set aside her busy financial accounting schedule to make room for creative expression. Playing the hand drum for the next hour and a half until her hands bruised began her forward return to a youthful passion. I asked her how it began to take shape.

> NR:, *"Growing up in Japan I was very open to Spirit, but of course I didn't know Jesus, or Papa God, or have any sort of personal accountability. But I was seeing Spirit all around, and music was right on the cusp of this. I had some piano training, but I wasn't very good.*

Around junior high, I decided to become a 'cool girl' instead of a 'spooky' one so I set the spiritual aside and joined the school band. As a freshman, I would set up the drum kit for the seniors, so I became familiar with it, but never got to play. I mostly played a snare with the brass band.

"I remember being so drawn to the beat, rather than to the melody. When I was a senior, some friends wanted to form a rock and roll band and asked me to play drums. I didn't really have any experience, but we had some fun doing Metallica cover tunes. I lasted through maybe two performances, and that was it for the next twenty-five years.

"Playing music wasn't feasible for me as I went to college and began a career and a family. My materialistic expectations weren't working out, no matter how hard I tried. I moved to the States, went through a messy divorce, and about eleven years ago, as a single mom, I turned my life around and slowly came back to spirituality. I began receiving a very heavy impartation from the Holy Spirit teaching me how to be with Him. Balancing spiritual life with family and the business world over the last ten years became too much. About a year ago I decided to step down from my day job to free up some time for contemplation.

"I have so much love for people, I could meet with different people for coffee all day long and never get tired of letting them know how Papa God sees them, how much He loves them. It's a gradual thing, this walk with Him, and He challenged me to let go of the outward responsibilities and reclaim the passionate things of my childhood. He was telling me it is not enough to love other people until I learn to love myself better. The feeling of being able to love others will always capped by the ability to love yourself.

"The process of self-discovery led me to realize I have always heard, always responded, to the beat of the drum. It was something linked to my early spirituality, and I had snuffed it out. When I came back from my mission trip to Australia, I approached Joel, the drummer at our church, for a lesson. So at forty-four years old, female, with time on my hands because my kids are grown, I sat down to learn about keeping time, about 4/4 beat, sixteenth notes, fills, dynamics.

"For me playing drums is not about playing drums; it is about receiving. God has given me this gift, and I received it early on, but I never owned it. It's about expressing the love He has for me, but it is so intimidating. Every single time it is mortifying. I am terrified of playing the loudest instrument in the room in

front of so many people, but I will go up there and play even though it is so scary to me. There is a sense of urgency, it just needs to come out.

"I get a lot of feedback from people, especially the ones who are not musically inclined. They seem to connect more with the spirit instead of the musical technicality. They come up to me and tell me they feel so blessed to see the boldness of somebody walking, as if they were naked, in front of the room and playing through the mortification.

"So my theme song has become, 'If I can do it, you can do it too'. It might not be drums for you, it might be anything else, but to know I can be inspiring to other people, gives me something too. He gives us a gift, and it is irrevocable. But we might not even know we have a gift until we see something in somebody else that might remind us of a desire, of an expression planted in our hearts.

"I always connected to music. It was like air— there was no way I could live without that—but I didn't always appreciate it as something personal to me. In thinking back, I realized that the beat, the drums and the bass, not the melody, is what I would pick up on, that's what moved in me. For me worship is loving on God, praising Him for being a Good Father, and the constant connection that I have comes to me in the beat.

"A week before I went on my first mission trip to Australia and wound up playing the hand drum in a worship circle, I snuck into the church at Fortuna at night and sat behind the drum set. I don't know what came over me; I don't know where the idea came from to do that. But since I had always heard the drum beat at the bottom of my heart, I wanted to touch the source. It was as if I had a stethoscope, and I was able to place it on God's heart and amplify it so everyone else could hear what I heard. I discovered it is at the core of who I am, of why I am here. I can see so much from my chair at the drum set, and even after hours and hours of playing, of repeating the same fundamental things, I don't want to leave that spot.

"Obedience has its own rhythm. Because I am so tenacious, and stubborn, He really had to knock me over to get me to change chairs. When I first came into the church, I never had time to be a new Christian because my husband was already in ministry—so it immediately became a thing of 'What can you do for us?'

"For years, I would do the finances until it became more of me than I am. He had to make a way for me to get back to listening to His Heart for me. His heartbeat is always changing. Sometimes it is very fast and I can hear spontaneously where I am supposed to play in the

song, but at other times, I realize I can't quite play what I'm hearing, so that gets me back to practicing, practicing, practicing.

"Everything for me starts out at night when my family goes to bed. I live maybe two minutes from the sanctuary at Fortuna Lifehouse, so I can be there by 9 o'clock and play until I have to sleep, maybe just past midnight. I love that time alone with Him in the building, and I feel like my time playing at night releases a blessing for the whole church."

I asked Naoko about the style of worship music known as soaking, which is more of an atmospheric appreciation than a lyric followed by a chorus type of music.

She answered with a sudden lift to her voice as if the subject were finally shifting away from her and onto her Lord. "I can soak in His presence with any kind of musical genre. If I am listening to jazz, the drumming is more on top of the kit, more cymbals, and more divergent rides. With rock, it's more on the bottom along with the bass. I am a light touch drummer, so I am really looking forward to exploring that—especially the classic jazz that has stood the test of time.

"God holds a preciousness for us that outshines any ideologies. I feel like the world is catching up and going to

that place, even if they have no clue as to Who He is, or what He is about. People can know all the good things He does for us without realizing a relationship with Him is the best part of the gift. People hesitate to make a commitment to a God that is larger than their ideas. A meditative culture aims to get past the thinking, into the experience, but if it doesn't allow for a living God, it is going to be too shallow—it will be limited to only what is natural to know.

"*When I allowed myself to become more awakened in my spirit, when I realized the Holy Spirit was more forceful, more insistent on connection, I knew I had a choice of commitment. Ever since I was a little child I was aware of the spiritual, but I was able to turn it on or turn it off. But now I understood I wasn't supposed to do that because He was giving me a chance to redeem all I had given up since my childhood.*

"*What began to happen was a soaking in of His presence every night from 10 p.m. to 2 a.m., which was like filling a cup of water that I could carry throughout my day and then bring back to Him at night to be refilled and refreshed with no interruption, no distraction. I am paying attention, and I want to be able to do it as an embrace anytime and anyplace. So I experiment with listening to different types of music as preparation to worship. Sometimes it is hard rock, or synthesizers, or jazz, or something from a foreign culture. I want to connect through that to His Spirit blowing through that type of music.*

"I need to be OK with not having the technical ability that I wish I had, or that I see other musicians have, or are striving toward. Sometimes it can get in the way of expressing Spirit, and I am so grateful that I can rest in Him, even relax, with where I am now. The connection to Him and other people is the purpose. t is not a by-product of technical ability. The joy that I see circulating the room when we are worshipping gives me courage to stay in the chair and just forget about time while I am keeping the time."

🎵🎵🎵

The interpersonal support of other musicians that Naoko refers to is manifest in the physical presence and playing of Noah Watkins, a childlike lightning rod of spiritual energy playing the bass as a bridge between the drumbeat and the melody. I sat with Noah to learn more about how head banging bass lines can create a reverent attitude. Judging by his ever-changing hairstyles and skinny jeans, I would place Noah as somewhere in his mid-twenties. He mentioned he used to be an atheist so I asked him what made him think he wasn't one now.

> NW: "Atheism is a life experience, and although it seems antithetical, it is a very religious outlook. What led me out of my atheism was an undeniable encounter with God. I love science, but wasn't basing either my atheism, or my faith on science. My life was a mess. I've been a musician since I was ten years old, mostly playing bass, and I played everywhere I could—even at church functions.
>
> "Where I met God, where I met Jesus, was playing at a church camp while I was coming down from a cocaine binge. It was about 4 a.m., and I was coming down hard and getting ready to end my life. I was listening to some music in my room, just feeling messed up, and I suddenly blurted out, 'God, if you're real, You need to come down here and save my life.'
>
> "I passed out, and when I woke up, I was still a little bit high from the day before—but we were supposed to play for the junior high camp. We got on stage to play and we played some fast songs, and then we somehow spontaneously flowed into a slower worship song. I felt it. I felt Jesus say to me, 'I love you.' I felt this calm in my heart, and I told myself it was just a few hours before that I was high and wanted to kill myself, and now the music

and the Spirit were just wrecking me. Chemically I may have still been unable to cry, I just couldn't make tears. But this encounter, it was my first sense of anything prophetic, a sense that I was going to be connected with God from that moment on. "I didn't read the Bible or anything like that. I still kind of struggle with that, but I started calling myself a Christian. Back in my room I would hook up my guitar, or my bass, to a bunch of pedals, and I would just jam for hours—literally just riffing for hours. Musicians will have a grid for this— when something is just so right about what you're playing, but it's beyond what you can normally do. It's outside, but it's inside, and I would feel this love in my heart like when I encountered God onstage. Music became my medium for connecting with God."

"I believe God is a creative God. That's pretty evident, and creating melodies became this way of communicating, of listening. I wouldn't say it was my best guitar playing, but it was just awesome, incredible riffs. I have some of them recorded. When I play them back, there's no disputing I'm a mediocre guitar player, but there is something there, there is an anointing riding on those moments."

The Proverbs of Solomon say in chapter 1 verse 33 NIV, " but whoever listens to Me will dwell in safety, and be at ease, without fear of harm." Listening to Noah talk gave proof to this promise; listening to Noah play bass is like taking a tour of a volcano that is on the verge of erupting. He jumps on chairs, he throws down a bottom sound that rattles the floorboards, he spins into the congregation like a Tasmanian dervish, and curls his tongue in some sort of salute to Alice Cooper, or KISS, while casting a beatific smile and a beam-me-up light from his clear eyes set on things above.

We talked about how different instruments, and instrumentalists, get stereotyped, or pigeonholed into expectations. The keyboard player is generally perceived as brainier than the drummer, especially if she wears glasses; the lead guitar player is always the crowd favorite, despite having no reach beyond a three-chord stairway to heaven; and the bass player, well the bass player is the moody one that probably has a good day job to afford being a part-time musician.

Noah came to the bass first, picking up the guitar to get a better notion of chords and theory, but the bass is his instrument of choice. He even intimates that the choice may have been the other way around. After I teased him that in the non-musical world bass would probably not get the top two or three religiously important slots, he leaned forward to explain his perception of the role of the bass being an evangelical tool.

> *NW: "I would suggest that you listen to any of the Red Hot Chili Peppers to get an experience of what the bass brings to the music. When I play the bass, and it may be due to a musical maturity, I'm not just listening for my line, but for the shape and direction of the whole song. I've said it before: The bass is the bridge between the beat and the melody. It's a huge role. The bass carries such a huge presence, frequency wise. If you look at the sound waves of the bass, they take up a lot of room, and they are very long. There travel the furthest of any sound waves. If you're outside a club in the street, all you can hear is the bass bumping. It might sound a little metaphysical, but the bass is what moves things. Your body's natural response to the bass is to move in the groove. Sonically, the bass takes up a huge realm, and spiritually I would say it does too. I don't know if I can directly answer that but it is what I'm after."*

I sensed Noah was seeking permission to explain something so personal that even trying to put it into words was a type of code break. Scripture says in Romans 8:26 NIV, "The Spirit helps in our weaknesses. We do not know what we ought to pray for, but the Spirit intercedes for us through wordless groanings which cannot be uttered."

Noah leaned forward as if bringing out a memory from somewhere in his bones. "There was a moment during Flood 50, our fifty continuous hours of praise festival, where the music was building to a point of guitar and drum crescendo. I was deliberately laying out, just listening to the whole room starting to swell, and I heard this low boom in my head like the Holy Spirit was directing me to slide down to my low B string and strum this powerful chord. I realized I was crying as my fingers hit the strings. It was so emotional, so powerful. It really set the worship set apart. The experiences I'm having, musically, and spiritually, are so new to me. I've never had anything like this happen to me before, and in a way, even though I'm in a band, it's kind of isolating.

"Most bass players talk about feeling the groove, but not in a way that acknowledges that it's spiritual. We just say it's groovy, but I believe God cannot be

separated from beauty. Any music, any art, that is powerful, intense, and fun . . . I feel like it is Holy Spirit directed. We just don't realize it is a spiritual thing going on, that God is in it.

"I was blessed with a really good teacher growing up in Michigan, and looking back, I see how that orchestrated where my approach is now on the bass. I wouldn't say I'm in the forefront of anything, but now I'm messing with a lot of pedaled delays while going up really high on the neck. There's a lot of genre identification with musicians, like, 'He's a gospel musician,' or 'He's a rock musician.' I don't like to split hairs like that. Who am I to say God isn't in heavy metal? I'm not going to put God in a box.

"For me, no matter where I'm at, in a church, or on a tour, I will never play differently. I'm going to show up with the same passion, the same drive to express myself. Biblically when Jesus died, God tore the curtain at the temple, destroying the separation between what's considered holy, and what's often known as secular. A lot of Christians aren't going to agree with me about that, but I believe my rocking out in front of five thousand people is just as intimate with God as me playing quietly by myself in my bedroom. I love playing for church, serving in that way, but I feel my life's call is to connect

people to each other through good music. The stuff I'm doing now is really heavy, and it's a lot of fun. It's supposed to give hope to people, but nobody listening to it would say, 'Oh, this is Christian music.'

"I love Jesus and I love heavy metal, and no matter what I do, people will be connected to God when they hear me play because I'm connected. You won't hear Jesus's name explicitly in my songs, but He's there because He's with me. Because I met Him while I was playing bass, it's easier for me to keep up in my walk with Him by playing music.

"I came out to California to do the Bethel School of Supernatural Discipleship, and while I was checking that out, I figured I should do the worship music. The school really helped me find my sound. I had just come off tour two days before school started, and when I went to audition I was all over the place. Steve Clark, the music leader at the school, was instrumental in my development. He heard me practicing and remarked that I had a very aggressive sound.

"I started to apologize for it, as if it would have no place in the worship music. He said, 'Not at all, there's power there. You should fill your sonic space and own that. Steward your sound, be responsible for that.'

"My attitude tends to pop out when I'm playing, whether I'm using a pick, or just my fingers. I have a meaty, sort of gritty sound, and if people only heard me and haven't met me they probably wouldn't imagine me to be a pretty scrawny kid from the Midwest. I don't currently have a fretless bass, but I love that sound.

"There's a player named Tony Franklin, and another guy, Juan Alvaretta, who plays with Mars Volto. They are the guys who inspire me on the fretless. Very beautiful, very intricate. When I'm rich and famous I'll definitely be getting into that. Jaco Pastorious is another modern fretless player who has probably melodically inspired every bass player alive today. Victor Wooten is another one who talks about music being a language, and if you want to be able to communicate with different types of people you have to learn how to speak sonically, through music. Not everybody loves metal the way I do, and you can't be limited to just jazz, or just country, and expect to get your point across. It's all about learning to be a better communicator.

"Music can create a very awesome dynamic, but typically church music has become very stale—not organic to the players themselves. The players do two or three songs, and they're done for the day. Very neutral, very cut and dry. The setting we play in, the circle with everyone

facing the center, is super lively. It's more like a family gathering around a table. You're able to lock in with the other musicians with just a smile or eye contact. The anticipation and appreciation can flow from person to person, or envelop the whole group, it's more like a jam band with God—you just lose track of time, as if a week really hasn't gone by since we last played. It's a continuum."

I asked Noah if familiarity with the setting and players worked against the Holy Ghost's ability to surprise him.

"It's crazy, but I'm continually drawn back to music as a means of communication with God. Not just expressing, but listening, conversing. And what makes it so personal and so fresh is that God knows how music works. I've been known to go into trances while I'm playing, seeking His presence . . . following a trail through songs we've played maybe a hundred times. Suddenly I'll lay a chord inversion that just reflects the connection of Jesus to the Father and His connection to us at the same time. The bridge between the drums and the melody communicates the bridge, the ladder, between heaven and earth. The frequency of the instrument attaches something sonically that our spirit yearns for like a deer panting for water.

"There is healing going on, and it's not just because we're happy to be playing together or rocking out. You see it in the street—people that come in because they caught the sound outside the building. As for myself, the battle with depression has no hold over me because this music just fills the cracks in my personality. Many times I feel we are doing what David did for Saul when he played his harp to rid Saul of his madness.

"One time there was such an anointing in the room, it was thick, powerful, and afterwards we got testimonies from people in the room. I remember this lady, you wouldn't call her a rocker by any means, but she said the music took hold of her as if it were Jesus's arms and just lifted weight after weight off her shoulders.

"Sometimes Steve Clark, the worship leader, will call an audible and say we have to stay in a particular section of the music because something is stirring in the room. Sometimes the whole band will be on the same page and pick up on it. We know it's the Holy Ghost, and we know it's in the music. We know it's not us doing anything special, but something special is going on. The truth is always in the intention. The reality of heaven allows us to choose how we'll respond to circumstances, to what people in the family are going through, to have a base line of gratitude even when stuff hits the fan. As a

player, my opportunity is to connect with God and set the table for His people to be with Him. It's not about being in a killer band, or playing really well together; it's about serving a purpose in the moment.

"A person might be gifted or talented, but if you don't steward that gift, if you don't choose to work at it, then you're only going to be riding a wave. You'll be limited to reacting, instead of responding. My personal checking point, my measure of being in tune, always begins with being thankful. Especially in the West, we're conditioned for what's next, the new thing, the prize, the consumable. I like to draw a halt to that by simply remembering what's good right now.

"The thing about musicians, about church musicians in particular is you're always pouring out. It's giving, giving, giving. Sometimes you have to slow down just to realize you need to rest. A lot of times, communicating is voicing, but learning to listen, to just be a worshipper in another part of the room while another player handles the bass gives me the chance to address what going on inside me with a certain sweetness. For me it's so vital to have my personal worship tank filled to the brim before I can even think about being part of somebody else's worship experience. In a way, it needs to be selfish in that I am only doing this for myself. I need to

connect with God for me. I love being part of the family, but I need to be His child before I can be anybody's friend, or brother.

"Just in living our life, we carry what worship gives us. That's what I love about Kingdom culture: It's a connecting vibe that's available to everyone. I don't care if people are Christian or not, there's an unheard spiritual song that everyone wants to be singing. No matter what I'm doing, because I have Life within me, I can make connection. I can make conversation with anyone. I don't have to speak Christianese. If Christians come to believe they have this hope within them, they can change the world just by having normal conversations wherever they are—at the paint store, at the bar, at the store. That's the beauty of the spiritual song that's running through my life. That's the gospel."

♫ ♫ ♫

Noah's reference to the story of David's harp playing led me to do a little Biblical research and, to my surprise, I learned that before David's victory over Goliath he was favored by King Saul for his musical ability to soothe the king's distressing spirit. The story is in the first book of Samuel chapter 16 and starts at verse 10 NIV, "Then Jesse made seven of his sons pass before Samuel. And Samuel said, 'The Lord has not chosen these' And he asked Jesse, Are all the young men present?' And Jesse answered, 'There remains the youngest, and there he is, keeping the sheep.' And Samuel said, 'Send and bring him. For we will not sit down till he comes here.' So Jesse sent for him and brought him in. Now the lad was ruddy, with bright eyes, and good looking. And the Lord said, 'Arise, anoint him, for this is the one!'

"Samuel took the horn of oil and anointed David in the midst of his brothers, and the Spirit of the Lord came upon David from that day forward. But the Spirit of the Lord departed from Saul and distress came over him and Saul's servants said to him, 'Let our master now command your servants to seek out a man who is a skillful player on the harp. And it shall be that he will play when this distressing spirit is upon you and you shall be well." So Saul sent his servants to provide a man who played skillfully and so it was whenever the distressing spirit came upon Saul that David would take a harp and play it. Then Saul would become refreshed and well and the distressing spirit would depart from him."

So far so good, but soon after David beheaded Goliath, Saul became jealous of the acclaim the people had for David and plotted to kill him. Saul threw a spear at David while he was playing the harp to alleviate Saul's distress, so it would appear there was nothing magical or automatic about the music's ability to calm his troubled mind. Another verse in the Bible, NIV Hebrews 11:6 states, "and without faith it is impossible to please God, because anyone who wants to come to God must believe both that He exists, and that He rewards those who earnestly seek him." I suggest that without faith, it is also impossible for God to please us as an explanation as to why Saul was no longer comforted by David's playing. If beauty is in the eye of the beholder, it stands to reason it is also in the ear.

🎵🎵🎵

I asked Justin Grimaldo, the lead guitarist of the core worship group at Lifehouse International, where he got his ears for music. He put on some background music to buy time for a response and crossed his arms to signify that he was in contemplation mode before smiling at what the memory stirred up.

> JG: "When I first started playing lead, I didn't know what I was doing. I was fourteen years old, and I actually lied to the leader of the youth group band and told him I played lead. I was playing rhythm, but so was everybody else in the band. I told him I was just like Santana, even though I had never held an electric guitar in my hands. I got to the audition and realized I didn't even know what a Marshall stack was. Yet, somehow, by the grace of God, they ignored the fact that I lied and let me in the band. I had a three-month waiting period to get it together, and they had some worship leaders at the big church who were amazing lead players. Over the next three or four years, I learned everything I could from them. At the time I was playing guitar in my garage up to eight hours a day, literally until my fingers bled. A lot of people say that as an exaggeration but I really did it. It got to be pretty obsessive. I would forget to eat; I wouldn't do my chores. My mom had to ground me from playing so much guitar.
>
> "It created a kind of problem because I never had access to that kind of voice before, for my spirit, like an electric guitar. I mean acoustic playing is fun and all, but I was hitting notes that unlocked whole new levels of

creativity in me. When I coupled that with some delays, reverb pedals, and overdrive, and built up my pedal board I started getting really cocky really fast. I started finding my identity in playing guitar, and because it was for a youth band I was encouraged to just shred all the time and really be aggressive. I quickly became the best player in that church. I just smoked guys who had been playing thirty years, which started to create some jealousy issues.

"One Sunday, when I was at the height of my cockiness, all my strings broke, and all the tubes on my amp blew out. I couldn't play. It became clear that it wasn't about me. From that day on, I began to look for ways I could compliment the band. I had been striving for attention in my identity as a really fast, really good guitar player, always ready for the guitar Olympics. Suddenly I saw a new role for me."

I asked if Justin had maybe been subconsciously aware his position needed adjustment as he seemed to quickly be able to attribute his technical difficulties to the Lord's guiding hand rather than a simple twist of fate.

"I could hardly consider the event as just coincidence, and that perspective probably helped me not get mad and belligerent about the whole thing. I remember standing there, unable to play, in front of six hundred

people, and sensing the Lord's presence like I had when I was a little child. Except that as a child, I was told to ignore all the spiritual stuff as it was probably demonic, and straight from Satan. I had a struggle in the middle of this potentially embarrassing circumstance to listen to what He was telling me, right in that moment, to choose to have an encounter with Him.

"That day helped me shape how I can encourage other people—whether it's people in the band I'm trying to support or people in the congregation who are sitting on the verge of an emotional or spiritual break through. As an example, sometimes I will see colors on my fretboard, illustrating certain chord inversions, and when I play them, I'll get told later it was that precise moment when somebody in the room was released from something binding them. So since the day I got slapped upside the head, I've been pursuing how I can facilitate other people's encounters with the Lord, like it's a frequency I can open into their brain, or into their heart. It doesn't even have to be all that holy; sometimes people just need to forget about their pain. I don't pretend that I only play to reach people for the Lord. I play to help people get release, to help them have fun.

"Because I was so cocky, I tuned in to how easily seasoned musicians can slip into self promotion. It doesn't

even have to come back to a spiritual thing. People love music, and I love being able to bring it to them. After I had that epic equipment failure, I met an acoustic worship leader, Kathryn Dunn-Moore, who started introducing me to a more spiritual ear for things. I started learning how to play to support her, and it was really new for me. I'd get ready to shred all over a particular part of the song because it was my turn, and she'd say, 'No, save that for later.' My initial reaction was, 'Who are you to tell me what to do? Don't put me in a box.'

"*At that same time, I began listening to Anthony Skinner, who plays with so many of my favorite guitar players—Jerry McPherson, Ran Jackson. Ran plays with a band called The Daylights and the way the guitar introduces the song became such a sensual thing. It taught me I no longer have to shred all the time, because with shredding there's no relationship with the song. Playing with Kat it started to make sense to compliment the song and move the relationship forward. Sometimes I remember being on the verge of some awesome power chord and pulling back to just play one note, with a little reverb on it—and it became the perfect thing and I loved it.*

"*I began listening to music to hear how the instruments complimented one another, or how they supported the vocals. One of the main bands for me is*

The Dave Matthews Band. They are so aware of where they fit, and they play so well. Sometimes a player will just stop and let the other guy fill the space. It was the same thing I was learning with Kat. I started playing a lot more just to serve the band at church, but I was always on reserve because the song structures were always A-A-B-C-A, and I began craving the more intuitional style that Kat was using. I started taking breaks from the other bands to follow Kat wherever she was playing, and then she got engaged and moved to England. I was playing with an awesome group of people, really concentrating on musicality, but I had lost my mentor. I remember looking over at the leader of the church band at the time and thinking, 'What is this we're doing here? Are we putting on a show?'

'It just wasn't fun for me anymore. I was really sensing and pursuing the Lord, the way Kat had been directing me, and I felt there was a block to my progress. I remember praying to God to send me somebody quick to play with, or I felt it was all going to come crashing down. About that time the church hired a guitar player from Texas, a guy named Nat Turner, and after sitting in with him for his first worship set I thought, 'This guy is amazing!'

"Nat did not like being boxed in, and he was definitely after the Lord in his music. Back then we had a dress code. We had to wear khaki pants and all these stupid clothes that none of us would ever wear otherwise. I was getting into arguments about it and here comes Nat, the newly hired leader, in jeans and a T-shirt. After that Sunday, the musicians started wearing normal clothes because expressing freedom was suddenly associated with the Savior of the universe.

"Nat invested in me a lot. He gave me my first pedal board, which I didn't even know existed. I would just leave my pedals all around on the ground. I had that pedal board for years, and it always reminded me that somebody invested in me. So recently I was able to invest in a younger player and pass it on. I told the story of how I came to have it and hoped it would unlock something in him like it did for me. That's becoming a real important part of the music for me, encouraging younger players. That means more to me than playing gigs, or whatever . . . helping someone build their dream.

"When I came to Lifehouse a few years ago I started learning about sonic spacing from Steve Clark. Because of where his voice goes melodically, I had to adapt my range in order not to clash with his pitch. The same thing with playing with a keyboard. If he plays low or

uses distortions, I don't want to muddy it up. So I have to look for a higher part, maybe an octave above his bass note. Over the years, learning to listen to the singers has been the biggest change in my playing. We have four or sometimes five different singers to work with. Some of them aren't that experienced with singing in a group, so it's up to us to make adjustments.

"There's another aspect that doesn't get much consideration in making the music sound good and that's the mixing board. People have this idea that a sound person just pushes a few buttons or rushes out of hiding to fix a squeaking microphone. But there's an art, a spiritual sensitivity to the blend in the room that really helps us as players. Especially since we're playing in the round, where we're facing each other, but we have our backs to the congregation, it's like we're gaining on something together, and the sound mixers help us get traction. Lately they've been experimenting with leaving vocal trails for just a note or two. Maybe Steve's singing in his falsetto, and a touch of echo gives a hint of a chorus behind him. It takes time to learn that, to learn the musicians and different singers, where they are likely to fit, or overlap in the sonic fabric. Without that person facilitating our sound, we would be screwed.

"I love watching Daniele Mammi back in the booth. He makes me so happy. He'll start jumping around because he put a new EQ setting on one of the singers and transfers the moment into something really bad ass, epic. Most people won't understand sonically what a mixer will do, because it's not like a drummer or a guitar player that you get to watch. But afterwards, I've heard from people that there was really something personal, something deep about part of the music. Technically, they don't know what it is, and I maybe do. I'm not trying to take away from the Spirit's influence on things, just the opposite. When He's moving in the room, He's moving in the sound booth too. Scientists are experimenting with how certain frequencies affect our brains, our emotions—like how a minor chord sounds more earthy. Danielle's learning some of that first hand by watching the reverb he adds to the keyboard, for just a split second, and the notes sweeten into this haunting texture.

"Sometimes we'll walk into the room, and even before we're playing, we'll feel a residual atmosphere, even a tension. We're still learning how to communicate with each other, and as weird as it sounds, we tend to hide our feelings or our sensitivities from each other, if for no other reason than just not wanting to deal with it. But that's

the best time to address what might be in the way of the music. So we have to become honest about being on the same page, about surrendering any normal versions of aggression or agenda.

"It takes a certain level of permission to admit that a fear of rejection is lurking about. I've come to play in the middle of personal heartbreaks, when I did not want to be there, did not want to play at all. The band picked up on it, like the family I expect them to be, and changed the whole set around to help me get release. Believe me we've had sessions where we just felt terrible about each other and the congregation will say, 'Oh you guys are so wonderful.' We'll smile and mutter, 'You don't know what you're talking about.' We've had crazy moments where we've played for two hours straight going after a particular level of grace like it's another dimension, and we're circling around this portal to other worlds."

I jokingly asked Justin if maybe they were experiencing the rock and roll version of Jacob's ladder.

"I'm kind of a sci-fi fanatic as well, and when the lights go down in Arcata, it really feels like a spaceship taking off. That's when I see a lot of colors, and I'll start bawling like the presence of the Lord is so thick there that we don't have to do anything but be willing to

receive. It's a whole other animal. We're not on stage in the traditional sense, and being in a circle, you can be alone with the Lord, and together with the room, at the same time. It's not random, and it rings true. The worship setting there is like everything is on the table.

"Lifehouse is the most freeing family I've ever been around. I hesitate to call it a church anymore because it's so much more than that—it's more like a tribe. It's just the beginning stages, too. What we're realizing is whatever success we're gaining, it's just the foundation for the people coming up after us."

♫ ♫ ♫

I left my conversation with Justin wanting to enroll is some sort of school where I might study the sound reasoning of sound waves. The foundation of aural aesthetics as a springboard for sonic spiritual discernment may someday prove to be a PhD-worthy area of study. I am not a born musician. Born again, sure, but I didn't start out as any sort of instrumentalist in my youth. When it was my turn to take piano lessons, the family sold the piano. I doubt that it was personally directed at me, the decision to trade away the not-quite-a-Steinway for a brown plaid couch, but I took it that way long before resentment was even a functional part of my vocabulary.

Consequently, all my musical motivation up to this point has been fueled by a desire for some measure of revenge, hence the saxophone. I grew up awfully white in Wisconsin. My hometown had zero black people. Hank Aaron, the last legitimate homerun king, had trouble trying to buy a home in the next town down from ours while he was a member of the World Series champion Milwaukee Braves. I didn't discover soul music, let alone jazz, until my older brother shipped off to Vietnam. After the war, he played *The Inflated Tear* album by Rahsaan Roland Kirk for me when I visited his apartment in the big city of Milwaukee. Rahsaan Roland Kirk has since become an absolute jazz hero of mine. Dennis, my brother, may have even heard Rahsaan play in Milwaukee. Because Dennis said Rahsaan was cool, he was cool to me.

Years later, I saw Rahsaan myself just a few months before he passed away. He had recovered enough from a stroke that paralyzed his left arm to play, but had his flutes and horns modified to play with one hand. In his heyday Rahsaan could play more than one horn simultaneously, not just honk and holler but play distinct pieces against each other, a feat compared to reading two books in different languages at the same time, aloud.

Music is considered a very extracurricular activity in most tightly budgeted educational systems. If you want to study music you will do it after school, and you will choose to do it instead of play competitive sports, since this is the only time slot allotted to furthering our cultural heritage. That decision brands you as a geek who would rather march in a costume borrowed from the big top than run around a quarter-mile track as fast as you can in little more than your underwear. I chose the latter.

And then came rock and roll, and live bands playing for the high school dance. Music had meaning—meaning it might get you the girl if you could play in the band or dance. Alas, my skill set was limited to running around a quarter-mile track in little more than my underwear. I didn't get the girl, but I definitely got the bug. My long-distance running teammate, the comedian Bobby Orvis, would sing mouth percussion licks as we rounded the hilly paths of coastal Wisconsin, setting the stage to inject me with avant garde jazz recordings when we met up again in college.

My destiny, it would appear, has often been aligned with the fringe. Poetry, jazz, political activism, organic diet, tai chi, my early adult interests cubed, rather than squared, my Eagle Scout, Catholic altar boy beginnings. The sound of a high choir cascading in a cathedral tuned my soul, my spiritual ears, as much as my enormous physical ones, to a music from above, to an acoustic voicing of the profoundly personal.

This inner bell of recognizing music as speaking to me rang so loud it took me many years to realize it was also a beckoning call for me to speak through music. I had fallen into the propaganda that only certain people were musicians and playing an instrument was only part of the qualifying procedure. Musicians had something—a walk, a talk, a way of moving in the world like bumble bees with a direct line to the best roses. Musicians had charisma, a notion easily exploited and promoted by our social medias and likely true through the ages if stories of Renaissance groupies swooning to the violins of classical Europe are to be believed.

The term, *charismatic*, as defined by my mother-in-law's copy of Random House Webster's Dictionary is "having a divinely conferred gift, or power". The definition goes on to say it characterizes Christians of various denominations who seek an ecstatic religious experience. I'm not faulting the Webster research teams for a typical English-speaking bias to ascribe what is more likely a universal phenomenon to a particular cultural group, as much as aiming for the divinely conferred as a more common target than we usually allow. The belief that musicians are born, not made, has some merit or the myth would not have survived this long. However, to suggest discipline and quality instruction cannot unlock the mysteries of melody and harmony is to sell the divine appointment short. Late bloomers still attract butterflies. Prodigy is welcome, but not required. Does not Wisdom cry out from the highest places in the city, "Whoever is simple, let him turn in here" (Proverbs 9:4, ESV).

Appreciating music adds dimension to being human. Producing music casts us from the shadows into the light of what the Divine has naturally, and supernaturally, designed for us as a connective tissue. The heart of why we matter to each other, and creation, is tied together like a rim shot on a snare drum to the downbeat. Sound reasoning might consider sound as a viable means of support for our soul, psyche, spirit, and general sense of self and society. When cultures or values clash (imagine a bus ride with loud country music and rap tunes coming out of opposing speakers), the result approaches what the apostle Paul called a clanging gong (1 Corinthians 13:1, NLT). The trick is not necessarily symmetry, or some high-speed blender of assimilation, but to find rest between resonance and resistance. Some stuff sucks, big time. Fact of life. Mediocrity is its own lack of reward. Discernment, sharper than any double-edged sword, encourages us to go to the heart, and intent of the songs we listen to; weak music weakens the mind.

Experimental experiences are like roots seeking new soil. Given the option, a living fiber will turn toward nutrients and away from stagnation. Our ears are designed to capture what the rest of our head might miss like the gigantic interstellar search antennae probing the outer regions for a sign of intelligent life. When something is indeed "music to our ears," we might note what is pleasing to us. Is it a reinforcing of the tried and true, are we being nudged to consider something just beyond our grasp, might the beat or pulse shake us from a dull reverie of day-in-day-out methodology? As a test of music as a universal language theory, I have been listening to random selections of foreign pop music: French, Brazilian, and Nigerian. I picture myself working a similar job to the ones I have now in a different country to try and get a feel of what the B-side of my life might be if I were born anywhere else. What would my coffee breaks be like in a world of sunshine? What would the commute become in the midst of a goat parade? Would my music teacher in that culture play something American to be exotic?

Of course it is all just daydream material; my passport hasn't got a fresh stamp in ages. But I wonder if I am becoming any more open to mystery by humming along to lyrics I don't understand.

The lifestyle of making music, the context of being a musician, is usually a condition of being in concert with other musicians, not necessarily on stage, but at least in cahoots. The relationship of the player to the instrument is the relationship to the self-made aural. The awareness employed in making a practiced, pleasing sound, or song, is a constantly moving discovery. Since most of the musicians we are exposed to are well known professionals, the connection between player and instrument is something we take for granted. A picture of John Coltrane without at least a mouthpiece cutting through the corner of the photo is awkward, more like a mug shot than a portrait. Bob Marley with his guitar is an image known worldwide as much as Michael Jordan with a basketball. Miles Davis is a possible exception to this not-quite-a-rule, because if anybody will be an exception to anything it will be Miles.

Our perception of the time spent with the instrument to cement our admiration of the musician is likely just a fraction of the time necessary to get the musician's experience to becoming noteworthy. An unspoken standard is that it takes 10,000 hours of disciplined practice to gain proficiency on any instrument. That equates to a little over four and half years of practicing six hours a day, three hundred and sixty-five days a year. Charlie Parker, Coltrane, and Jimmy Heath, to name a few, probably doubled that in addition to performing, touring, and recording. But where is the threshold between becoming a beginning music student and being a continual student of personal musical progression? Is it 100 hours? 1000? Why do people pick up an instrument for the first time, and why do we put them down as failed experiments, frivolous whims if they don't lead to American Idol ?

Our culture has created a dichotomy between music and ordinary perception and expression. Talent is presented as a separating principle rather than something that binds us together. Consider how normal it is for us to remark that someone else is talented and how foreign it feels to suggest, or flat out admit, that we ourselves are talented.

There is a conspiracy at work, and I hesitate to guess who it benefits. My suspicion is it is entirely demonic and of the same stripe as the serpent's taunt in the Garden of Eden that we can only know what God knows by disobeying Him. The notion that some people can't carry a tune in a wheelbarrow has just enough credence to make it dangerous, leaving the heavy lifting to too few of us to realize the hills are indeed alive with the sound of music. This same antithetical reasoning delegates the direct perception of the divine to the polemic air of mystics, fanatics, and the pure of heart.

There is something to popping our fingers that connects us to the outreaching hand of God in Michelangelo's *Creation of Adam*. It is such a given that music is part and parcel of Divine planning that Paul mentions, in his first letter to the Corinthians, the mystery will be revealed: "In a moment, in the twinkling of an eye, at the last trumpet. For the trumpet will sound, and the dead will be raised imperishable, and we shall be changed" (1 Corinthians 15:52, ESV).

But why wait for the last trumpet when there are so many great trumpeters alive today who are as willing to change our perspective as they are to change keys? Music is not just a consumable, copyrighted product. Compositions exist to tie time to the timeless, to give inkling to incarnate compassion, to create a proof of the profundity we harbor as our true home. The shallowness of the lowest popular denominator dominating our airwaves does not refute the grand scale anymore than a bank of heat lamps would keep us inside on a sunny day in June.

The power of music to inspire was so feared by the fourth century church fathers that they conspired to ban it from church life lest it rival their less-than-awesome view of God. It wasn't until Pope Gregory canonized the chant that worship music came back into the fold. A casual survey of what passes as American Christian worship today would suggest that innocuity is the highest possible virtue, reducing the hope of glory to a harmony more reminiscent of a Beach Boys cover band than Bach, Brahms, or Beethoven. It was Bach's experimenting with a well-tempered scale that gave birth to improvisational compositions of discovery. The expanding cosmos was unlocked when music breached the narrow mind.

Sun Ra's Infinite Research Arkestra reminds us, through otherworldly cacophonic theatrical theorizing, that *Space is the Place*. A juxtaposition of his eclectic electric keyboards with Hildegard von Bingen's *Canticles of Ecstasy* brings us full circle into the wheels Ezekiel saw in the middle of the air. (Ezekiel 1:19, NLV).

Attempts to prove God do not necessarily gain God's approval. The Dark Ages were rife with problematic theological certainties, not the least of which was a theme that everything worth knowing about God, or nature, was already known, and the only point of any intellectual search was to reinforce the prevailing assumptions of the day. The high concept of "what if" was left for tinkerers, or delegated to the fool's gold of alchemy. The progression of curved glass lenses from simple magnifier to spectacle, to microscope, to telescope is an apt analogy of what happens when people begin to look at things differently, to see things more as they are, rather than as they seem. Faith never asked to be set against reason and scientific advancement should have been cause for celebratory revelation of His marvelous ways, as it certainly was for many of the individual faithful making the discoveries that led to the Age of Enlightenment.

Tuning the clavichord, a predecessor of our modern day piano, was one arena that saw, or rather heard, the drama between the predetermined and the possible play out. Early harmonics were based around the vocal strata of the male choruses toning the Gregorian chants. The projection of perfect major thirds should have logically led to a perfect octave, but when the thirds were stacked together, the result was a dissonance that couldn't be mathematically accounted for, or easily tolerated.

Tuners cheated nature and retuned the dissonance over all the ensuing intervals to make the octave true. The tuners took matters into their own ears and once the instruments began to sound better, it became necessary that they play better as well. The discovery that pure octave based scales could be made from any point catapulted music beyond the limited range of the male voicing, just as the stars became closer by telescopic observation. The realm of the inner ear became magnified to approach the heavenlies by a combination of increased technology and unbridled curiosity.

A note is a tone fixed to a page of music. The tone played is sensed as a presence in the room, an emotional exhibitor, an exhalation. This bit of disturbed airwave reaches us where we live. Our private dance, our encore behind the shower curtain, our alternate future, our reconstructed past . . . it all vibrates as a knowable joy lubricating the bones of our story. If we were ever to divide into tribes and board the designated starships of our destinies, the choice of music—more than politics or ethnicity—would define our trajectory. One nation under the groove. The something new under the sun is our part in the choir. The still small voice is still a voice. Faith comes by hearing.

We tell each other, "That doesn't sound like you," when a disbelief about ourselves takes a position it hasn't earned. The rhythm of our life is more than a routine pattern of coffee intake and punching clocks. The room to improvise, to improve, is an ever expansive opportunity.

The simple act of singing leads us to uncover joy as a personal tuning fork. When things are humming, we feel as free as the birds of the air. The correction of an off-note is only a half step, up or down, in any scale. It may be the easiest adjustment in all the creative arts. Similarly when we catch ourselves lying, especially to ourselves, we can undo the hurt with a replacement truth.

Paul says, in 1 Corinthians 14:15, NKJV, "What is *the conclusion* then? I will pray with the spirit, and I will also pray with the understanding. I will sing with the spirit, and I will also sing with the understanding." Prayer and singing are linked. They are not different sides of the same coin, but they are divine currencies. The logical world scoffs at one, and dismisses the other. Folks who don't have a prayer are rarely, if ever, in an enviable position. When Moses crossed the parted Red Sea he declared, "The Lord is my strength and song!" (Exodus 15:2, KJV). He wasn't just whistling Dixie. Switching the vocal intention, and intensity, from a normal speaking voice to a singing voice puts a capital B in our Being. To serenade is to persuade, no matter how high the balcony, or the moon.

My efforts of raising the musical bar are personal, mostly solitary experiments. I'm an amateur, a student. I woodshed just to have a place to call my own. I draw on whom I've heard, whom I've met for context, and project myself into a great hall housing an audience of One. I listen and pretend someone else is listening, playing along, answering me in glissando, making one moment more real than the next.

The make believe makes me believe I'm headed toward something, a performance, an exchange, an insight. I face my ticking clock and count the sweep of the second hand as my conductor's baton. *One-E-And-Uh*. Four notes per beat. Sixty beats per minute. A concerted effort to stay on it for a minute at a time. The flight of fancy lifts from repeated launchings. Upbeat. Downbeat. Beats in the middle beating me into pulsing anticipation.

I played cowbell for an African dance class for a few months. I was mostly tolerable. My clave was

Caucasian to the max, even with sunglasses. I play my horn as an outgrowth of that, sticking a note, a pattern here, there, and here again. My biggest imaginary thrill would be to play in a horn section dropping R&B riffs. Because I don't sustain melodies very well, I like to make tags as if to say, "This is it. This is why we're alive. This. This. And this." My points of reference skip along the surface of reality like a stone hoping to delay sinking into the lake by hopping to it.

Musical buoyancy has a bounce and I'm about to test mine by playing in public with a heavy metal bassist and drummer for a set during fifty hours of continuous praise music our church sponsors every six months. We have a ninety-minute to jam and little in common besides joy and enthusiasm. Our set list to date consists of me interjecting some spirituals—"Swing Low Sweet Chariot" and "Sometimes I Feel Like a Motherless Child"— over their manic measuring. If we were better musicians—or more accurately, if I were a better musician—the premise might hold more promise than presumption. We've practiced twice and may get one more chance to cohere before folks get to hear us. The basic idea is: If you can't make the band, make your own band.

Music theory is just that until a note is struck. We can't teach the world to sing until we sing our own song. Realizing we each have one, a song, a voice, requires some exploratory faith. I hope every sound I make with my horn is pleasing, musical. While it is true we are differently gifted in terms of innate musical abilities, it is equally true that an untapped talent is nothing to just bury as a consequence of being busy in the real world. The gruffest voice can still soothe the savaging of our self-doubt. There is a cruelty that melody confronts. Joining the morning bird song gives our day a hope, a suppliance.

Usually when an orchestra assembles, the first request is for a tuning note. An A. One A has a frequency of 440 Hz, another 220 Hz, or 110 Hz, or 55Hz, 880 Hz, 1760 Hz, and so on. There is an A for everybody. If we compare our A unfavorably to someone else's as a permanent condition we suffer, but when we match our A, a harmony is generated. The strength of a sound is not the most important quality. The willingness to bend, to adapt, is what lends it pleasing to the ear. Learning to listen is learning to sing. Listening to music is the beginning of making music, as it allows the construction of sound as a personal possibility. We enlarge ourselves by joining the chorus, and the choir of angels makes room for us on the head of a pin. Our souls are designed to perceive and project perspective. Mystics have often spoke of a third eye; how they missed a third ear is beyond me.

The space between notes played is called a rest. God rested on the seventh day, but on the eighth, and every day since, He's been on the bandstand, in the practice room, at the rehearsal hall, in the recording studio, on the radio. Creation has moved on. To paraphrase the song What The World Needs Now , "There are mountains and hillsides enough to climb." Few of us will become professional musicians or singers, but we can all lend something to the melodies and rhythms of our shared experience. Music teaches. Music reaches. Creation does not stand pat, or apart, from our Creator.

Daniel J Levitin explains in his excellent book, *This Is Your Brain On Music* that the receptors in our brain don't just recognize the frequencies that we qualify as music, the brain actually matches the frequency so if amplifiers were connected to that region of the brain, it would broadcast the perceived sound pitch by pitch. By contrast, a similar test on the visual receptors would not project any color, shape, or shade of a perceived object. Sound perception, and production of sound, connect more parts of the brain's function than any other tasks we present to the mysterious ocean we house in our skulls. We are all wired to be musically perceptive, productive, and prolific.

Scripture refers to making new songs all the way from Exodus to the Book of Revelation. Even if the only words we use are "Holy, Holy, Holy," or "Halleluiah!" there is no end to the variations possible to make glad our heart. We are not puppets being pulled by a string, but there is an exponential joy in our strings being played together. I hope we can agree music is a bonding agent and, let's not forget, our popular culture suggested, just a few decades ago, that when the extraterrestrials encounter us they will want a set of black and white keys to communicate.

Suggesting a higher purpose to music doesn't mean the low notes should not be funky. Dance and trance don't rhyme by chance. George Clinton's *Mothership Connection* transposes into "Swing Down, Sweet Chariot." It's all church music if you're a star child. Musical discipline isn't necessarily any more spiritual than dental or mental hygiene, but an overlooked aspect of the original sin is delegating music into an exclusive territory of the talented and acclaimed. Lucifer couldn't share the stage with either God or us, the new fangled sons and daughters of the Most High. Doesn't play well with others doesn't begin to explain the damage the devil's introduction of ego (sin) into the world has done, but grace prevails, and a sound demonstration of that is our singing a new song.

When does a new musical expression become a song? Jerry Coker, jazz instructor and performer extraordinaire, suggests in his classic book, *Improvising Jazz*, that the establishment of a definite motif is what lays a foundation in the ears of the listener for a tune to become a song. He quotes Richard Brown, pianist and jazz instructor at Yale with this insight about song formation. RB "I believe it should be a basic principle to use repetition, rather than variety-but not too much. The listener is constantly making predictions about what is coming next and must come out right about 50 percent of the time. If the listener is too successful in predicting the music becomes boring, and if it is too difficult to predict, the musical turns and outcomes the listener will give up, and label the music as disorganized."[1]

The new song we sing onto ourselves, and before the Lord, could be a lyrical, conscious intonation redeeming a personal misconception we harbor about ourselves and our relationship to the Divine. "I can't sing" is perhaps our most common self-delusion. When scripture exhorts us to sing a new song unto the Lord, there isn't an asterisk with a footnote excusing us from the exercise. While it may be painfully true that some of us do not sing very well, it shouldn't obscure the notion that we can all be made more well by singing. In the world of alternate

---

[1] Improvising Jazz by Jerry Coker Copyright 1964 Prentice Hall, page 15.

therapies, stroke victims are sometimes counseled to sing nursery rhymes as a way to re-engage damaged nerve connections in the brain.

"Just listen to yourself!" is the admonition our exasperated friends might give us when we're being especially stupid. In a gentler tone the same message could become sagacious advice. Taking a gentler tone with ourselves is an aid to fulfilling Christ's commandment to love our neighbors as ourselves, especially if our self-criticism has become especially harsh.

There is a supernatural grace to declaring positive expectations for ourselves. It is not wishful thinking to give voice to a loving parent's desire for his or her children, especially if the alternative is repeating the accusations of the deceiver under the guise of being practical. Music doesn't naturally gravitate toward insult, although I have to admit Johnny Paycheck's "Take This Job and Shove It" has a stake at cultural significance. Imagine the swagger we might carry through the day if, like relief pitchers in baseball, we had a theme song that piped in every time we applied ourselves to the task of the day. "Eye of the Tiger" might be a bit much for taking out the trash or vacuuming the living room, but would it hurt to hum "Good Morning Starshine" while we brushed our teeth?

We all sang and hummed naturally as children, and somewhere along the line, we became convinced singing was only for singers. Imagine where our language skills may be languishing if we decided speaking was only for speakers. To begin again, fresh as the mercy of a morning dew, all that is required is to find a note in the back of our throat and push it forward on a breath of air. We don't have to name it, we don't have to make a song of it. A single note expressed has its heart in the ear of God. "From your mouth to God's ear!" is a popular way of supporting hopes that seem unrealistic, but it is also an accurate map of the course our internal music takes when it takes to the air. The one syllable chant of *Om* is just one simple example of giving devotional voice a place in our life. If that's "too Eastern religious" for you, change the spelling to *Home* until you can work up enough air support to try a multisyllabic expression like Halleluiah.

Terms like "spiritual" and "musical" just need an extra l to be all inclusive, sort've like the extra all in all y'all makes a plurality. Music all. Spirit all. I once asked my pastor to distinguish between scat singing like Louis Armstrong and speaking in tongues. He reckoned Mr. Armstrong had more fun and may have been closer to the truth of the matter than we give him credit for. Either way, it's not the textual veracity of what we sing that matters as much as our willingness to make a joyful noise. Jesus said we are to receive the Kingdom of God as a little child (Mark 10:15). Could it be Our Father wants to make googly eyes at us while we gurgle up praise like bubbles in a glass of milk? I'm not suggesting we all make plans to have a concert at Carnegie Hall a life's goal, but maybe we could make our ordinary environments ring like high-ceilinged cathedrals with just a hand clap and a holler.

Our brain has more capability to distinguish sounds than any other stimulus. We can follow a friend's conversation in a crowded, echoing airport while listening for a departing flight announcement, and tap our foot to a passing beat box without batting an eye. While multi-tasking, in some cases, may be a mask for inattention, we can decipher and maintain a memory for innumerable aural inputs, especially music. The advertising industry has rendered this ability down to its lowest, and all too common denominator, with the barrage of jingles our Western culture endures. If we would but endear ourselves musically, personally, and collectively to any sense of well-being, worship, or wonder, our ears might pioneer a frontier of expressive connectivity. We say there is much to be said about this or that; it is equally true, if not more so, that there is much to be sung.

Daily fitness regimens often include exercise, diet, sometimes rest, meditation, or other recuperative components such as massage. Incorporating song is usually limited to an electronic device tuned to a workout loop. Belting out a tune while we pump iron may add a very real dimension to increasing our muscle tone. Sole music is walking the talk with a beat. Such a progressive procession could give us the chance to be the different drummer the world is waiting for, or at least our neighborhood.

I'd love to read a report of tombstone carvers reporting a sudden uptick in inscribing "He Always Had a Song in His Heart." The legacy we're here to leave plays better with a sound track. The song says, "We Shall Overcome." Take note that a song is carrying the message that carries us forward.

Music may well be the closest thing to the sound of love in our lives. Certainly a lyricist would think so. Loving the sounds we make is a highly favorable option. Ask any parent if they fuss over the diction and tonal qualities of a child learning to speak. While there is a marked exhilaration when bah-*gah-goo-boo* becomes "Mama" or "Papa," the beginning non-sensible syllables delight the listener for many months. Considering ourselves as babes in the woodshed should free us from any overly critical expectation of musical prowess as a prerequisite for singing praise.

We rarely excuse ourselves from singing "Happy Birthday" because we lack musical training—we even join in to sing for strangers when a candle-ridden cake floats above our heads in a restaurant. Self-consciousness is a weak and distant cousin of consciousness, and as we realize our Father/Mother God/Creator is clapping along with our *Baba-Goo-Goos* we may relax into an imbedded groove programmed to accentuate the linkage between mind-spirit-soul-body-family-congregation and community. When the saints go marching in is a great song to take outside the walls of whatever isolation we harbor as being the extent of our influence and compassion.

Singing can only bring the joy that is brought to us and, if the joy of the Lord is our strength (Nehemiah 8:10), it stands to reason that the enemy of our souls would choose to weaken us by impinging on our song. Again, the happy babble of pre-speech infants is our most vibrant clue as to the high purpose of song in our lives. A child's squeal of delight, even at a ceiling piercing pitch and unfathomable decibel level, is part of proud parenting. Causing a single note to express all that we feel, treasure, and wish to proclaim is exactly where the task of praise begins.

Soul singers and horn players intrinsically know how to cut through the demonic fog and realign our attention to what's possible. I'll admit I'm showing my instrumental bias since none other than Chuck

Berry reminds us that Johnny B. Goode could play that guitar just like ringing a bell. The point is, as we begin to sing more often, more and more things will make us feel like singing.

If the first rule of writing is that what we write must improve on a blank page—or if you prefer, a painting must bring organized color to an empty canvas—then a song should disturb the quiet surrounding it without being disturbing. The only singing lesson I ever took, which is not to say the only one I'll ever need, had me standing in a corner of a room, nose to plaster, listening to the sound of my voice bouncing back into the room. I felt an uncanny sense of amplification and identification with the acoustics of the room. Without learning anything else that day I had a new sense of my sound, my voice, being an atmospheric conditioner to a specific space. I might not yet have had the courage or conviction to fill the room, but I could certainly hold my own in the corner. I felt like a boxer practicing my upper cuts and jabs before turning around to face the center of the ring.

Selina Wesley was the gospel choir director at The House of Refuge Christian Fellowship in Santa Rosa California when my wife and I first started attending church in the mid '90s. My wife, Trey, was quickly recruited to sing soprano-alto in the choir and in the smaller praise combo. As male voices were scarce, I was inserted as a bass voice and taught how to do the Baptist sway and clap at the same time. No small feat. The choir, of course, sang at church services, but also performed in public venues and joined forces with the all-male choir at San Quentin State Prison a few times a year. Selina's patience and professionalism were often tried, and her frequent expressions of, "Lord, have mercy!" were as much testimony of exasperation as prayer.

I asked Selina if her musical ability came more from self discovery or from the encouragement of others as she was growing up.

SW: "I've been singing since I was three years old, and in my family, that wasn't unusual. I enjoyed singing, especially with my dad in the choir at my grandfather's church. I realized pretty early on that I could carry a tune and sang every day right into grammar school, where I was constantly told I sang too loud. I never understood that, but I kept on singing right up until I became a teenager and people that knew me and heard me sing in church began to tell me they believed God had really anointed me to sing.

"The sounds that come out when I'm singing really give me joy. It doesn't have to do with Christianity per se, but when I'm feeling down, singing lifts me up. I never thought about it til I was much older, but singing helped me be happy on the inside. The more I sang, the stronger that sense of being happier when I sang became, and I started mimicking the people I heard singing around me, especially my dad.

"I can sing anything I hear, but I have to find my place in the music. If it sounds right I go with it. I'm actually pretty shy. When I get around other singers that can really do it well, I tend to draw back and feel a little intimidated. I grow more, as a singer and as a person, by rising to the challenge. It's one reason I like to sing in different venues—weddings, concerts, or visiting other churches. If it's a new audience I can come at it with less expectation of how I am supposed to sound and surprise myself. Many a time I've stood back and wondered, "Where did that come from?"

"I recently was asked to sing at my cousin's funeral. I really wanted to shine, to be able to express my love for him at my very best. I found a place in the music where I could come out rather jazzy in my inflection and my phrasing. I was not expecting to do that—usually I'm more traditional—but I was in a deep place of hurt. I let myself go into it emotionally because my concentration was on just trying to make it through the song. I have felt it when the Lord takes over the song, and when that happens I honestly don't even know what happens.

"To me, singing to the Lord, singing onto Him alone . . . I tend to be more relaxed, more free spiritually. The doors to my heart and soul are more open, and it's reflected in the tone and the sound quality. When I'm singing about Him, I'm trying to reach somebody. I'm trying to get a thought out, more than trying to get a feeling across. I'm focusing on the recipient, so the song is not about me, personally, but more on what it's trying to say.

"I will say that when my father passed away, and then my mother, and my sister, all in a short time, the only way I could make it through was to sing. I was so sick to my stomach—it's still hard for me to talk about it without breaking down—but I remember as a kid, as a teenager I would hear my dad in his prayer closet,

which was really our bathroom, speaking in tongues, and there was a musical quality to it. The expression that came out of that is something deeper than I knew how to do. When I was grieving the loss of my family, I couldn't talk about it, I couldn't write anything down. All I knew to do, for my wellness to begin, was to sing. All I could do was call out, "Jesus! Jesus!" I couldn't even make words or remember a song. I had a melody in my heart, just two notes, enough to carry His Name. That song began to lift me enough to get out of bed. It gave me enough that I could have a smile, just for that moment. Because I was able to sing His Name out loud, and feel Him, I knew I wasn't, and wouldn't be, forsaken.

"I need to sing to not feel lost in this world, and if I don't sing for a while. . . . It's like exercise, it's either use it or lose it. It starts with opening my mouth to try and find a note. I encourage people, even if it's just humming, to try and find a note. We can never know what our inner voice sounds like until we let it out. When I hear myself recorded I'm often surprised, because I don't believe I sound as good as I do, and it helps me perfect my tone. I have a contralto range, so even though I imagine my voice as being really high, like a soprano, it's not. So hearing it reminds me to give breath to the bottom, to the whole range of my voice. I've learned I have to stretch my voice

past my comfort level. I know where I can go vocally to be heard over another individual, but it's more exciting to learn how to be heard together in a harmony.

"Right now I'm having fun singing with children. We take turns mimicking each other, and it's amazing. They can hit my tone, they can hit my pitch. Children have musical ability, and if someone doesn't squash it, if we would just let them be, they wouldn't develop a fear of singing. People only develop a fear of something, of singing, because someone steps in and tells them they can't do it. With me, my teachers always told my parents I could sing, but I was too loud. When I tried to adjust to their criticism, it took the joy out of singing. I didn't want to do it anymore. Thank God the encouragement of my parents was stronger than what my so-called teachers were saying about it.

I asked Selina if she had a pet peeve about the way people were conditioned about musical abilities.

"If I have one thing that I would say to people, it's don't lose yourself when you listen to other people who sing better than you do. Comparing yourself to a professional or someone who is more talented is an easy way to get discouraged, but your part in the harmony is your part, nobody else can do it. If you are humble and

honest, if you can get yourself out of your own way, what God has put in you will come through.

"Recently, my cousin, who has a high degree of musicality, challenged me to begin to verbalize my own feelings, my own ideas, into songs, to write my own lyrics. I don't know how to write melodies, so he suggested I pair up with someone on an acoustic guitar. I love singing a capella, but to bring it, my voice, into an acoustic range with another instrument is a really hard thing to do, to stay in that key.

"I think people who sing along with their phones, with their ear buds in, have no idea what they really sound like, and it's scary to be exposed to be out there. For me it really helps to know the song, to have it down cold, and so, as I'm beginning to experiment with my own material, I'm really curious to see if the anointing that I feel in music will carry over into making up the words."

CHAPTER FIVE

Taking Notes Seriously

♪♪♪

I am playing in public today for the first time since last year's jazz camp. The event is called Flood 50, a continuous fifty hours of worship conducted every six months by my home church. I've played a few sets before in this venue, usually by myself in the wee, wee hours of the morning. A mix of Coltrane ballads and spirituals gave me something relatively reverent to cover the ninety minutes, but mostly exposed my musical limitations, even if it did give a justifiable representation of instrumentals as legitimate praise music.

Today I'm being recruited to play in a Latin setting with a conga player and freeform vocalist. Because I play a saxophone, I'm thought of as a jazz player. My plan is to play sparsely, in time. and in tune to support the vocalists and interact with the conga player.

The irony is that I have not yet considered any spiritual preparation outside of an "O, Lord, don't let me screw this up" prayer. The willingness, the desire to worship, especially instrumentally, doesn't forgive presumption in the place of preparation.

To balance my anxiety against my excitement for the opportunity I've been listening to players in a Latin mode while I work at my day job, and have been playing along with recordings when I get home. Horn players are often advised to sing the lyrics to a song through their instrument as a means of tying into the emotional content of the song. While I was mulling this over I remembered my teacher, Tony Pagano, telling me to think of the three-syllable word, beau-ti-ful, as a pacing device for playing triplets. The word em-pa-thy came to me today as a similar device that could be useful in today's setting.

A rehearsal, or two, may have gone a long way to settling my nerves without endangering the free spontaneous flow of ideas, but time constraints didn't allow for it. I'm left to trust the time I've put in on my horn and to examine my motives. Showboating is a sure way to sink any hope of connecting with other people. Nonetheless, there is a loud and frenetic cry in my heart, as well as a tempered, even whispered, solemnity.

The advice is always to play with heart to hearts afresh. Sincerity supersedes cleverness. Scripture says, "If you keep silent at a time like this relief and deliverance . . . will arise from another place... who knows but that you have come into this . . . position for such a time as this" (Esther 4:14, NIV). My Pastor used to tease me that, "until a real Apostle shows up, you're it." I'm taking the same approach to represent the saxophone community until Gabriel switches horns.

The event is a mini-circus of painters, dancers, musicians, the occasional poet, floor-wandering prophets, prayer tents, and folks just soaking in a supernaturally charged spiritual atmosphere for freedom. The rules of religious structure are wiped clear of the atmosphere to allow a personal, and interpersonal, sensing of the presence of the Holy

Spirit as the Supreme Party Animal. The joy of the Lord is the strength of the gathering and the joy gathers spiritual steam from one session to the next. Amateurs share the performing space with more polished and organized groups without a hierarchical sense of warm-up acts and headliners.

Some of the sets might register as heretical to folks accustomed to defining worship as a sing-a-long. The norm being heavy metal bassists busting out ballads to a controlled frenzy of hand drummers, blending into a pixie-voiced call-and-answer chorus after a tribal gathering of First Nation dancers set the tone with a reverberating chant, knocking on heaven's door like the persistent widow waking an indifferent judge from a midnight's slumber (Luke 18). Creative Christian Chaos.

My part, as the elder statesman, is to add reverence sonically with just a hint of *Soul Train* resonance. I plead, with my horn, for God to send us a more complete horn section, so I don't have to fill up more space than I am technically able. To be true to the moment is all that's required. I pray, to find the right key and then use that key to loose what is loosed in heaven. A simple jump note might unlock a dislocated sense of wonder in a heart too shy to scream in public. A cascade, a trill, might unfurl a twirl in the back of the room where shadows beg for the light of day.

It's a little weird being a mid-Western white boy trying to interject what has been invested in me by Providence. But when the shoe fits, everybody's a Cinderella at the ball, and the Prince of Peace holds out His hand for the next dance. I am so grateful to have practiced long enough to fit the bill that I nearly lose my place in the singer's pacing, and wail away at the wall of restriction we sometimes put between ourselves and the throne room of God. Politeness in the power of expression is peace keeping in action. Leaving space for love is how we grace ourselves, and to paraphrase Sun Ra, "Grace is the Place."

Perhaps singers know better than anyone what Saint Francis meant by his plea to be made an instrument of the Lord's peace. The singer's body is the soundboard, the microphone is just part of the surrounding air. The Passion translation of the Bible presents an interesting take on the matter in Psalm

8:2, "You have built a stronghold by the song of babies. Strength rises up with the chorus of singing children. This kind of praise has the power to shut the Satan's mouth. Childlike worship will silence the madness of those who oppose you."

The book of James elaborates on the power of the tongue as a small flame that can set an entire forest ablaze. Singing, being after all personally amplified speech, is powerful fan to that burning desire to be heard, and perhaps understood. Lyrics, coupled with music, become resonant residents of our mind, soul, and even our body. Pop songs of our youth, advertising jingles, and other trivial tunes are more likely lodged in our consciousness by the sheer act of repetition than the masterpieces of our time. Conscious listening choices may be as much a spiritual discipline as sitting in silent prayer. If we are to believe internet advertising, listening, even subconsciously, to EEG vibrations can cure us of self-doubt and early hair loss.

The audience of One is all-inclusive. We play on to the Divine Ear that fills the room, much like the tongues of fire did in days of old. Flood 50 is broadcast in a live stream across several continents. Sometimes the image is shaky, sometimes the sound breaks up, but the safety the sanctuary offers wraps like a dancing blanket about the head and shoulders of the folks gathered in the praise building. My perspective is colored by looking out over the neck of my saxophone. To get a better feel for the experience, I asked one of the participants for some perspective.

🎵🎵🎵

Haley Gurr is a praise singer. This would be evident even if you never heard her sing because her smile and demeanor are simply uplifting. I imagined there must be something more complex around her sense of the sounds from within so I asked her what are the components of singing with God rather than to God.

> *HG: "The Lord told me when I was in my teens that I was made to worship. Singing at Flood 50 is a butterfly-like experience for me. I usually pick a time to sing early in the morning, when few people are awake. It gives me a sense that His ear is just for me, just for that moment. I feel myself fly above my worries, song by song, for the whole hour and a half set. My tears and my*

worship are just between me and Jesus. It is the most precious time with the Lord I have.

"I dedicate myself to worshipping . . . and doubt, fear, failure, all the other worries, lose their grip on my focus. I look upon Jesus and feel invited into peace, to look on how big and good God is, and be able to make sounds that tell that story even more than the words of the songs do. How can that not be good?"

CHAPTER SIX

Brighter Moments

♫ ♫ ♫

I made it back to sax camp, the Inside:Outside Retreat held at Victor Wooten's camp in Only, Tennessee in the summer of 2018. The reunion with the friends I had made in the jazz community was heavenly, a live real-time convergence of the saints marching in. There wasn't any particular musical reason for folks to be so welcoming at my return. I suspect that somehow my joy at being in that number translated to extended handshakes and fist bumps. The event itself, even after four years, seems to be forever fledgling, the idea being to provide a natural setting to explore the sounds of creating an intentional and international community of saxophone players.

The standard joke is that it is impossible to tell, just by looking, if a camper is a saxophonist or part of the kitchen crew. The exception to this rule is Bob Franceschini. Even at one hundred paces, it is impossible to imagine his presence as anything other than the epitome of a horn player. The beret, the goatee, and the forward curve of his shoulders all contribute to his stature, but it is the ever present bop of his internal beat that projects a jazz essence into a room as soon as he enters. Bob is one of the founders of the retreat and tours with Bela Fleck and Victor Wooten, the camp's host.

His slant on instruction centers on the enharmonic connection of the saxophone to the human body. Starting at the tip of the mouthpiece, through the neck, down the long trunk to the ringing bell at the bottom of it all, Bob traces the movement of air and idea, of body and soul, from concept to concerted completion in a language of scientific mysticism. He seemed a perfect candidate to talk with about the sound of spirit. We settled down across a picnic table next to the long B-B-Q pit in back of the kitchen. The woods were alive with birds, the yard was buzzing with players preparing for their next session, and the tepid coffee reminded us we were on bivouac.

A helicopter buzzed over the camp as we started to chat, creating an adventure movie- atmosphere for us to huddle into conversation as if we were co-conspirators in a mastermind plot to bring world changing music out of the backwoods of Tennessee. I asked Bob if the phrase, "Sound of Spirit" itself rang any bells for him.

> *BF: "I go through moments, I have these times, when my logic, my scientific side of my brain says it's all horseshit. It's not real, it's an emotional thing. But then I'll have a gig or something, and be so moved, I'll feel so much spirit in the music, that it completely erases that thought and I'll think,* There's more to this existence than what we can see, there's more here than what we can prove. *It can't be so cold, the universe can't be such a cold thing that it's just material. There has to be something else, a realm that we're dealing with that's beyond the logical mind. I've had so many unexplainable experiences through music that after a while I asked myself, "Why am I fighting this?"*

After the fiftieth or sixtieth time that something, some connection, happened through music, I was open to a spirit being associated with music, within the vibration, within the sound that connects us and can't be explained. Here's a recent example, there's a kid that comes to camp . . . he started coming when he was eleven, which is right around the time he began losing his sight. By the time he was sixteen he had lost his sight entirely, but he had so much energy, so much light inside him. It leaves you wondering, "How can someone who has lost so much be so calm, be so full of life?"

There's a trail back here called Luke's Loop, that he helped cut into the hillside, blind. He can walk all up and down this camp without any assistance; he even does skateboarding! He's from Atlanta and he went to college around here. When we came back to camp last year, he had just come from a mission trip to raise money for kids to get musical instruments, because he felt so strongly that kids all over the world deserve an opportunity to learn to play music. You know, just a tremendous human being. Around here people are so touched by his performance.

He sings now, and he plays bass. He accompanies himself on the bass and writes his own compositions. So I've been helping him with his record, and about two weeks after he came to camp and sang, he fell ill. It turned out the brain tumor that caused his blindness had come back. He was hospitalized here in Nashville; they had to remove the front part of his skull to remove the tumor. Victor Wooten and I went down to see him, but it was funny because I was thinking maybe I should bring my horn and play for him, but he's in a coma. As soon as I see Victor, he says, "You should bring your horn."

So I brought it and when we got to the hospital, well Luke looked terrible. I mean he looked like a monster—so much of his face, his head, was just gone. On my way over I was thinking about what I should play. When his mom saw me, she encouraged me to play, but I didn't have a song or anything worked out. t was just music coming out almost like a gospely type of hymn. Now, telling the story, I'm getting emotional, but when I was playing I was just in it, and all of a sudden, in his full voice, Luke says, "Now I can be happy."

We all just looked at each other, and as the nurses came running in all his levels on the monitors started popping! This wasn't just physical, it wasn't just that his ears heard music, it touched him on a deep level. We played for him again that week, Victor and I. Victor brought an amp, and shortly after that he was up. He's having a hard time, but he's up. He's walking again.

They never thought he would be able to get out of bed, let alone walk. It's unbelievable.

Just that one exchange, that one thing . . . first of all, the music was just coming out of my horn. I didn't even feel like I was playing. Usually I'm thinking about something—a particular chord change, or I'm trying to remember a melody—but this was just flowing, this beautiful hymn. I should have recorded it. The power of music to heal somebody; it's beyond us. I can't justify saying it was just a coincidence that Luke woke up at that moment.

So I've had moments like that, but a simpler thing would be when my mom was dying, my wife played her some of her favorite music. I mean I didn't even think of it. We're in this cold hospital. It's all silent, like eerie silent. There's no music, no anything. My wife brought in headphones and played her some Eydie Gorme, some of her favorite stuff. At that point my mom had pretty advanced cancer; she was on really strong meds. But for that hour, that hour and a half, she was transported out of that situation. She was singing, she was imaging herself dancing with her husband. It had to be spiritual, because physically she wouldn't have been capable of any of that. It was so good to see the change in her.

Those are the kind of things that make me think there's more. Recently, getting into the nerdy science of subatomic level research, they're finding that beneath the atomic structure is sound. Everything is built on vibration. Even gravity is now being thought of as not a source of its own, but a response to vibration, to resonance, to sound, which produces a magnetism. The earth itself has a resonating frequency. They used to think the core of the earth was this iron ball that would affect gravity, but that's not the case. The center isn't solid— it's in flux, it's movement.

My understanding of the Superstring theory is that the universe is made up of these tiny pre-particles vibrating in harmonic partials that create everything. It makes sense to me to call it Spirit, this other knowledge that may be too heavy for us to grasp at just yet. There are certain things we can't answer. Why can't we define what consciousness is—with all the knowledge we already have we remain clueless. Even as our technology increases, we're losing touch with some things that previous cultures understood, elements of personal cosmology. We dismiss the deep, and I think it is arrogant to do so.

It reflects the direction of our society. If you take a look at the music industry, the way the musicians are getting shortchanged at every turn, the respect for the creative is diminished. It's reflective of the loss we exhibit for people who are sensitive to this sort of thing."

Our outdoor conversation was laced with the random sounds of saxophonists walking by with riffs, licks, and tones representing a traffic of ideas. The green valley bowl of grass at the center of camp filled, emptied, and refilled with the music of the moment approaching the timeless. The instructions passed on were not just technical fingerings, or aural advice on *embouchures* and memorizing charts, as much as cultural placements, examples of how the sounds of the woods and the sounds of the ghetto embellish each other. Bob smiled at the sunlight bouncing from the bell rims of the passing horns as we talked about where his initial interest in music came from.

BF:" I grew up in a funky neighborhood, early '70s, very mixed, racially. Our apartment was atop a nightclub, an all black nightclub, El Dante's. My bedroom was right over the jukebox and I think at night the music was going right into my head. My parents said when I was little I used to dance in my crib when certain songs came on the radio.

My parents are from Puerto Rico, so they listened to that kind of music, and our apartment was an older building, so the walls were very thick. The building was full of people from the Caribbean. My parents would blast the radio, and the people would come over to dance in our apartment."My parents were dancers, they would go to the Palladium to dance to Tito Puente. So music was just everywhere in my house, in my neighborhood, but nobody in my family was a professional musician.

When I was about eleven, or twelve, I started listening to pop records, and I was drawn in by the sax solos. When I got to junior high school, I went in for the music classes and started playing the saxophone. It went pretty well; within a few weeks I was actually playing the saxophone. It was crazy. I played a little piano when I was young, nothing serious. My friend's aunt was giving me lessons; she played this Latin stuff and was really good. But as I started really studying the saxophone, I was after saxophone music and that, of course, led to jazz. My dad bought me a couple collections of saxophone music and I was immediately drawn in deeper to the music.

In school it was a release for me, a kind of escape. The music program at junior high had two great teachers; Martin Kirschenbaum and Justin DiCioccio I'm still in touch with them. They encouraged me to audition for a the High School of Music and Arts, now called La

Guardia High School.. I got hooked up with another teacher who coached me to play better to prepare for the audition. I got in, and by that time I was hooked. There were some great players in that school, and they were all trying to be jazz players. I didn't know what I was doing, I didn't know any music theory or anything. I won't say I was faking it. I mean I didn't know what I was doing, but I was able to play convincingly.

I listened to R&B players, funk players. I still do today, but the jazz sound is the saxophone sound I was after. At my parents' house, they were playing a lot of pop music, and Boots Randolph was a sax player on a lot of those records. I love that dude. I wish I had gotten to see him. But I'll tell you a weird thing about the spirit of music. The people that I've gotten to go on tour with . . . I feel like I've made connections to them, through the music before I ever got to meet them. Not in a calculated way; it wasn't like I decided I wanted to go on tour with somebody and started listening to everything they had recorded, it was more like I was moved in a special way that only made sense after I hooked up with them. I've had five, or six different tours that came to me that way, where I sensed while listening to the music that I was going to become involved in some way.

I asked Bob about good music being a force for good in the world, as John Coltrane's poem, "A Love Supreme," suggests. He told me a story about first hearing the sax/poem as a kid.

BF: "I stumbled upon it. I was listening to the record and looking at the liner notes. I realized the words of the poem were lining up, note for note, with his playing. There was no doubt Coltrane was communicating the source of the force. That is his legacy."

♫ ♫ ♫

As mentioned before, the Inside:Outside Retreat is the brainstorm of three saxophonists, all named Bob. Bob Hemenger would be just as at home in a wilderness survival camp as he is at a music camp. He represents the nature wing of the retreat's curriculum and finds as much thrill in finding a couple of rattlesnakes mating on a footpath as in helping a young player negotiate a solo on Wayne Shorter's composition, "Footprints."

We had a challenging time just finding the time to sit down and chat. Being a camp director means every minute from dawn to pre-dawn is a co-ordination of agendas, arrangements, and unseen angels. We finally plunked down in the business office in the midst of an inventory count which proved to be a fortunate setting as I got one of the last camp T-shirts in my size. Bob reiterated the perspective of spirit being a vibrational essence.

BH: "The Sound of Spirit." I like that. I think that's really one of the gifts, one of the roles we musicians are charged with, of touching that depth, of feeling that and letting it come through us, making the ordinary sacred. I would love to say I have an answer as to how music chooses us. I do feel for me, personally, music was something that I just got at a very young age. I know some players where that wasn't the case. Even in my own two daughters, one really wanted desperately to play and worked really hard to get there, but there was an element she had to supply herself. The other one was a lot like me and had it since she was like three years old. I do know we can learn and grow into becoming better musicians, but I can't say why some folks have the talent for it in the first place.

I think we get glimpses throughout our lives of something that's much bigger than us, and you can call that whatever you want. I like to call it The Great Mystery. In fact in my life's path right now, I'm not interested in defining any of it. When I was younger I wanted to figure everything out, have a name for everything. We were talking about why some people are attracted to jazz and some people are more comfortable with country. This isn't a judgment thing, where one is better than the other, but it may be some sort of sophistication attribute that is internal that connects us in some way to the music that makes the most sense for us, that satisfies something on our way to Nirvana, or whatever you want to call our destiny.

When something moves me—whether it's in music, or just in life, in nature—I want to feel it and touch that feeling, to hold on to it as long as I can. One way I do that is to be grateful for it, to thank Whomever is doing the moving, of creating that space in us that relates to vibration. Music, nature, my children, these are the ways I can reach into the Divine and know something that's much too wonderful to just be about me. Somehow it just shows up in those moments, and music is such an avenue for those types of things.

I have a friend, Ellen Tolland, we call her ET for short. She's run hospitality for a jazz festival out in Telluride for some thirty years now. ET has a saying about why she loves taking care of musicians, why she will bend over backwards to help them. She says, "God's energy is kind of like alternate current and direct current, and if we got it directly, all of the time, it would be too much for us, so He put musicians in place to receive it and convert it to an alternate current.

I really like that, and maybe it helps explain some things.

🎜 🎜 🎜

I left Bob to the business of organizing the final morning of the retreat and watched the patterns of campers getting ready to go home—of the performers setting the stage for the send off, of the kitchen staff whipping up another tremendous breakfast and packing to-go lunches for the departing. I marveled at the function of this temporary, international village in the middle of the Tennessee woods. Conferences are a dime a dozen—well usually hundreds of dollars—in any walk of life. Every profession, or special interest group finds value in gathering and disseminating information. I don't know if a worldwide gathering of plumbers would address the challenges of circulating the living waters, I would certainly hope so, but this camp has a way of imparting the party atmosphere with as much education, encouragement as it does entertainment, or dare I say enlightenment.

I bumped into another of "the Bobs," Bob Reynolds, in the shuffle of suitcases and buses and arranged to talk more by phone when we got home, It only took four months to hook up because one of us—I'll let you guess who—was busy with a world tour with the Grammy-award-winning band Snarky Puppy Because I'm trying, perhaps a little too hard, to present music as some sort of divinely inspired antidote to the world's problems, I asked Mr. Reynolds about the notion of music taming the savage beast. I should point out that anyone who looks at a picture, or a video, of Bob playing tenor saxophone automatically mutters, "Savage Beast!"

He dove right into the deep part of the concept.

BR:" The definition of music is organized sound, so there's nothing inherently soothing about music itself. If somebody plays a bunch of notes and it's not organized, it's not music; it's just sound. The soothing part . . . I'm thinking about my daughter's school where the kids and parents play a concert, and it's not necessarily soothing because it's rough. So it's more the sublime moments people are thinking about—the Yo-Yo Ma concert—not the kid who just picked up a cello two months ago. So is it music, or is it the refinement of music? I expect its more the life experiences and choices of a Yo-Yo Ma—I'm just using him as an example—to use all that he has available to make the most beautiful and intriguing organized sound possible to pull out all the triggers that have an emotional effect on the listener.

I'll give you another example. My son hasn't seen the musical, Wicked, *the huge musical on Broadway. I haven't seen it either, but there's a particular song in the musical that I've heard many, many times. It's called, "Defying Gravity." I recommend that people listen to it because the music is so strong. The music is so manipulative it nearly makes me break down and cry every time I hear it.*

So my son comes into the room while we're listening to the song, and he knows all the parts of the story. He's not seen the play, but he says, "This where the witch is taking off." He's made all the associations of the story to the moments in the music just from listening to the song, while my wife or daughter tell him the story.

There are these triggers in music, and when they are used by somebody who really knows how to use them, that's where you get this "calming the violent soul" scenario. So it's not just the music itself that does it, it's in the hands, and the ear of the composer, or performer who does it.

The other night we did a performance and a woman who was there for the first time came up to us afterwards. She was telling us how she was moved by the performance. Now it's not that she was moved by my sax solo or how the group was performing the material. I think she was moved by a combination of the material and the way the music was moving in us as we played it.

This gets me back to the point about the music being manipulative. These moments in music, you're aiming for them spontaneously, but you never know if you'll get there, when they'll happen. It's weird, but the way you prepare for them is by letting go of the self-serving ego kind of thing and trying , in the best as possible way, to give yourself over to the other musicians, and just walk away into the unknown, completely immersed in the surrounding moment. That's the blissful thing, this inclusive immersion. The audience is recognizing the connection with the other people on stage is not contrived.

The experience is as spontaneous for the individual, me, playing as it is for the group playing together, and for the audience. I'm nervous before every show because I know I would like that to happen at every show. I also know I can't force it. There's so much not knowing involved. I don't know how well I'm going to play, I don't know how the show is going to go down, I don't know how well we're going to play together.

Generally, after the first set, I get a sense of relief that it's going well, that those moments we're after are available. It's a little bit different than, say, performing a piece by let's say, Beethoven, and you know by the thirteenth page there is an epic moment and as long as you play it right you will contribute to that euphoric result, because it's on the paper, the written page.

It gets back to what I was saying about the extreme mastery of the musician being a factor in the desired effect. If you play "Ode To Joy," you'll get to joy, the quality of the orchestra is the variable, not the written music. The stuff I do is riskier; I don't know beforehand if it will work. This is all a long-winded way of saying the soothing power of music is when the music is rendered skillfully; that's when organized sound can be the most effective emotionally."

Bob and I got into a short side topic of discussing Amy Winehouse's horn section as being an example of the right note at the right time, crossing from historically accurate reference to tight horn arrangements since the 1950s to being a futuristic projection of sound. The tragic toll drugs and alcohol extract from the musicians making the music, and the folks who enjoy it, is the counterfeit to the healing power of music. Listeners, and players, come to music to satisfy a hunger, to be taken care of, to be sustained, encouraged, delighted, and entertained. The professional, whether it is a musician, a writer, or a dentist, focuses on the crafting of the art to be ready in the moment to deliver what the inspiration suggests is needed.

> BR, *"When I'm in the practice room, I don't spend one minute on lofty concepts. It's all I can do to focus on the minutia of the craft so that when I get to playing with the group or I get to the stage, I can play without having to think about any of those things. The spiritual side is in the moment when I have no idea what's coming, what connections to the other players, or the audience is available, because of the personal preparation. That's the Yin and the Yang of it for me. If you give honor to the preparation, it's more likely to be an honorable performance."*

Music exemplifies the ability to sway people, to encourage them to dance to the beat of a different drummer. I asked Bob if he ever converted someone to becoming a jazz enthusiast.

>BR *"I never consciously set out to convert anyone to the genre, but I have brought people to hear specific players they may not have come across on their own. There was a club called Smalls in New York City, and when I lived there, I invited some people who weren't likely to even remotely listen to jazz to come down on a Wednesday night to hear Joshua Redman with the drummer Brian Blade. When they came out of the show, they were as moved as someone coming from a Baptist-Pentecostal church service.*

>*"They weren't moved by the genre of jazz; they were moved by talented people making incredible music. They could feel what the music did, and they became curious about it and wanted to find out who this guy was who was making this music, and they wanted to check it out. For that matter, I don't know if I've converted myself to the genre of jazz. It's always been more of a search for individuals making musical moments that moves me. Often I find them in that genre, but a lot of times I don't. I just watched a Quincy Jones documentary and there's a moment in there when he's talking about music. He was hosting a symposium in the '90s trying to get the hip-hop communities to stop killing each other. He said he came*

from a time when there were only two kinds of music, good or bad; it wasn't about genres.

"Harmony is a set of sounds I like juxtaposing against another possible set of sounds to try and get the hairs on the back of the neck to stand up. Quincy said the hardest part of composing was scraping away the bullshit, the stuff you already know, to get to the real stuff. It's a process of shedding layers of pretension. I can't compose unless I'm chasing something exciting, something that intrigues me.

"The chance we take is if something works from inside of us as performers, it may well move the listener as well because that's the world we live in—a bunch of humans responding to each other. That's the realm of the most beautiful music. I don't think you can start out that way, of self-indulging a group of notes to move the masses, and come out with something meaningful, something resonant. To take it back to the bandstand, when we have those moments with each other, the audience shares in them, but we can't pretend. We don't put on airs, it takes enough air just to blow the horn."

♪♪♪

One problem I was glad to have at the Inside:Outside Retreat was finding so many people to talk with about my project. Part of me sensed everyone at the camp would have something to add to my research, but the camp's schedule limited me to who I could sit with and visit between rehearsals, workshops, and performances. Mary Hendershott, a Kansan who now resides in Burkino Faso, West Africa, was happy to park under a shade tree and discuss her world view of music. She plays flute, saxophone, and piano, and works as an ethnomusicologist in Africa for the past twenty-five years.

I asked Mary to demystify the term ethnomusicologist.

MH:" If you think about anthropology, and culture, and society from a musical perspective, you discover ways in which music impacts daily life as well as history. Some of us are more interested in research of indigenous instruments and tracing them into antiquity, and some of us are looking more at the application of music to the way people live. For me, it is more about the present. What's happening now and what changes have been brought about, and how.

Globalization has brought about commercial and pop influences, but on a local level, it is so much more integral into people's lives. An easy way to be introduced into the functioning of a society, or a neighborhood, is to hear what kind of music they play for celebrations, for weddings, for initiations, births, graduations, or even funerals. There is often a musical style, or a particular instrumentation for that particular event.

Work songs, for example, are much more likely to include improvisation, and if the work is domestic, let's say grinding grain or corn, the improvising answer to the chorus is likely to be ever praise, or criticism of the lady's husband. The liberty to express herself is protected in the musical form; she can say things in that format that she would never be allowed to say outside of a song.

The work itself, the sound and rhythm of the tools become the music, so any kind of group activity, like say pounding a new floor, has a song form. The participation of the group is not just about getting the job done, but also in getting it to sound good, to fit together".

I brought Mary up to speed with the way musicians from the camp had responded to my Sound of Spirit inquiries. Some folks gravitate more towards the Sound part of the equation, and some light up more with the notion of Spirit. I wondered if an ethno-musicologist might have an easier time of bridging both worlds.

MH: That's a very interesting question, especially for a musicologist. One of the premises is when you go into to listen to the music people are making, the music is culturally defined. We, as listeners, may not know what the people making that music are expressing. The music, the sound waves themselves, don't inherently have a meaning, but we as humans give it meaning.

In the research I did I found there's a certain note on the balafon . . . when that is played in a certain pattern, the whole village will take note, even wake up in the middle of the night, because something has happened, maybe somebody died. Because they grow up in that culture they hear the sound and the spirit conveyed. That's my starting place. I know some people will disagree with that, and say they are separate things, but I've had experience with that from musical cultures all over the world.

In a little bit different direction, I've been thinking about performing music—specifically, what happens in our own heart, body, and space when we're playing. I played in a church setting for a few years. Then I got a chance to play in more traditionally artistic spaces around town. One of those places was at a restaurant atop of an open-air terrace where it was very dark on this particular night. The thought that was going through me as I was playing was: God's Spirit is light, there is no darkness in Him and I'm playing, in this setting, in His light.

Now at this club, for a lack of a better term, there are prostitutes at the bar who were watching us play. I was looking at this young girl as I was playing. She was all made up; she just had that available look. I looked at her and just smiled and her face just lit up. So as I'm playing I'm thinking of all this and sensing, praying, really, that He would draw her near. I don't even remember what group I was playing with, or what songs we were playing. I do remember a lot of Americans were at the club that evening. Afterwards, the girl came up to me and said, "I wish I could feel the joy you have, in doing what you do."

For me, that, in a nutshell, is how we are to function in the world around us. Music is this wonderful, creative thing that we have been given as part of our adventure. And what we have in our heart, in our spirit is what we have to share. The joy in our heart comes through in various ways. Songs are a way of marking that. Through playing music, through playing jazz, we learn to love this expression. In high school nobody really told me this could be fun, or even that this is doable.

Later, in college I gained more ability to get into the heart of it, and it became something to keep alive for life.

♫ ♫ ♫

The camp lunch bell suddenly rang over our heads as if to remind us that even food for thought requires calories. Psalm 23 reminds the Lord sets a table for us in the presence of our enemies. He does a pretty nice job in the company of friends as well. The spread at camp from the kitchen collective of John Schopp makes me wonder if my next book should be *God and Gumbo*.

The comings and goings of camp sometimes hinted at ongoing connections. At other times, the sense of "now or never" permeated the chance conversations between jam sessions. The opportunity to talk with Juan Carlos Rollan came upon a midnight clear as he had a few minutes to grab a bench under the stars before an early morning flight swooped him from camp back to his busy performing and teaching schedule in Florida.

Juan warned me that he was an untwistable subject and subject to profanity. His eyes were a least as bright as the overhead celestial lights, and his readiness to talk suggested I'd better get my seat belt on. I told him the working title of my project was the *Sound of Spirit* and gave him a downbeat.

> *JCR: I have a story at the ready. I was at a jam session at a place called Les Partner's Lounge in Clearwater, Florida, I was maybe nineteen at the time. The house rhythm section was a guy named Kevin Bales on piano, Steve Worstein on drums, and a guy named Ricky Ravelo on bass. These guys were much older than me, much more seasoned and amazing musicians. So I had the pleasure of cutting my teeth playing in jam sessions with these guys. I had been listening to a lot of Charlie Parker and Cannonball Adderley coming up, but around this time I was getting into the classical John Coltrane Quartet stuff:* A Love Supreme, Crescent, *not quite* Interstellar Space.
>
> *I had this inner emotional connection, I actually was moved to tears. I broke down crying to his recording "Alabama." It still makes me tremble today to talk about the feeling I had listening to that song. I remember reading about the history of that song—the bombing of a Black church that killed four schoolgirls.*
>
> *That was the first intense, emotional connection that I felt to jazz music. The rest of the scene was like, "Look at those cool shades, and listen to those slick lines,*

I want to get into this shit." It was all this self-serving desire, "I want those chops. I want to make all those cool sounds." It was all mechanical; just the pretty things about the saxophone that we all tend to like. But this was deeper to the meaning than anything I had ever experienced.

So I'm at this jam session, and maybe this story doesn't tie immediately into the Coltrane reference, but I was really trying to tap into those types of harmonies. I was also much more athletic then and had much more lung capacity. I was a young bull, full of fiery energy.

So, we're at the jam session, and we're playing like a medium tempo modal things, maybe it was Impressions, *I don't even remember. Here I am, looking to explore, and this is the only time this has ever happened in my life: I entered into this crazy trance like state. I kid you not, man. I remember it as vividly as if it were happening right now. It felt like my consciousness left my shell, and I was literally hovering over my body, over the bandstand, listening to myself play.*

It was such an intense experience I'll never forget it. It hasn't happened to me since. So whenever I hear people talk about astral projection, I listen, because I don't think it's bullshit. As far as "Spirit," I think I believe that we're comprised of three parts—mind, body, and spirit. It makes sense, but spirit is a hard thing to quantify. The mind you can measure, because you lose it once in awhile. The body lets you know when it hurts when you bump into furniture. But the spirit is the intangible."

Our conversation began to draw attention from late night stragglers heading back to their cabins and campers who wanted to say good-bye to Juan before he left. The concepts of spiritual, or religious traditions, ramped up the animation and volume level of our discussion, almost like a drummer was pushing us toward a chorus and crescendo. Juan's family history as a first generation Cuban gave a setting for his spiritual path. He mentioned his Mom still believes in God, Christ, and Mary, but doesn't go around rubbing the rosary. His Dad got away from the traditional beliefs when he went to live in New York City. His father was witnessed to by an Evangelical when he moved to South Carolina and began reading the Bible again, but from a Protestant perspective.

JCR: I don't remember too much, as I was a young child, but my Dad progressed enough to where he was called on to read the Scriptures from the pulpit. You know, be a lay leader, that sort of thing. Unfortunately, well maybe, that church was an aggressive culty kind of place, and if my parents went on vacation, or wanted some time to themselves, the church leaders would call and harass them about their loyalties. It got creepy so from that point the family never really went for anything organized. I, on the other hand, when I got to be older started hearing my friends talking about Christianity, I don't know if it was the style of the approach, or some deficiency in the theology, but every time somebody tried to tell me about the Christ, it always rubbed me the wrong way.

I had some devout friends who never beat me over the head with it. When I went to college at UNF as a jazz major, they were there too, as part of the choral crowd. One girl, Lisa, became friends with a trumpet player and an incredible piano player, Scott Klibbetts. Those guys started playing at a church in a contemporary praise band.

Now I was real hard-hearted at the time, but one day Scott, who was also my buddy, started talking to me about Jesus. The way he did it was actually kind of cool. He was asking me if I knew the details of the crucifixion. I knew something about a crown of thorns, but he basically spoke the Mel Gibson movie to me, and it hit me, it was heavy. Scott was telling me He did that for me and through that conversation it made me start thinking, and I asked him if they needed a sax player for the church band.

I had a really good time playing there for like three or four years, it was like United Methodist, but it was super cool, and I really loved the pastor too, really cool guy. I joined the church. It was really small, met in a rental unit in a shopping mall. I even got qualified to go door to door with these guys, doing the whole tract-witnessing thing.

At the time, I was developing romantic feelings for the girl, Lisa, behind this whole thing. I proclaimed myself to her, and in retrospect, she was really kind of sweet about it. But in so many words, she said being a musician meant I wouldn't be able to provide the kind of stability she was looking for. She went on the say I wasn't in God's plan for her. My relationship with her and the whole church thing gradually got exposed to me as a sham, like just a club for like-minded social climbers."

The philosophical theological bends of our midnight ramblings drifted a little closer to the Ornette Coleman side of things as we marveled at the futility of trying to measure the divine by human standards. The cultivation of the positive, in relation to people we love, and people it is difficult to love, is the ongoing improvisation Juan ascribes to. As soon as fear enters into the methodology of conversation, or conversion, it becomes a con, a manipulation. Refuting the tenets of a religion, of a mind view, doesn't short circuit the relationship of Creator to the creative process we enter, and that mystery is the music singing through Juan's life, the rebel without a pause.

♫ ♫ ♫

Steve Davit is an improviser's improviser. Part of his repertoire is conniving non-players to take up instruments on the fly and make music by the seat of a collective pair of pants. His recordings include work with Marian Hill as well as his solo projects

> *SD: I've never put the sound of spirit as a term to my music before, but I have endeavored towards those moments when I'm playing to not being limited to just being myself. I'm not sure if I'm channeling something that's inside of me or something that's coming through me, but that non-thinking moment, that not-worrying vessel for something bigger than myself is a continuous*

aim in my music, if not my life. It's called lots of things. I've read scientific explanations for flow as one way of describing, or measuring, but in music, at least, and it's a lot more than that.

The push is to be slightly above your skill level, so the boundaries you're exploring are close enough to territories you're comfortable with—so there's less anxiety about being able to meet the challenge. Improvisation is interesting because we are spontaneously setting that challenge in front of us and, in a group setting, inviting others to join us, which increases the complexity of the challenge. Improving our technique is a vital preparation for that kind of exchange, but it is only one component.

I've had interesting improvisations with people I've never met before, but I find the more transcendent moments happen with a person I know very well, and we already have an unspoken connection. The communication that allows, that back and forth creativity, is something we really don't plan out, as much as we encourage each other into an allowed possibility. The aspect of spirit is interesting because, as we know, not everyone is religious. I do have family members who make music and believe that God is a big part of their creative process. I don't necessarily think of music in those terms, but I can respect people who do.

I think it was Stephen Pressfield who said back in ancient Rome people were believed to have a genius—not that they were geniuses, but like a genie. We have spiritual beings sort of assigned to us that help us create.

I like that idea. You could call it a muse—something else that is there to help you—but it's your responsibility to show up for it. It's not always going to happen, every improvisation isn't the greatest or even better than the last one. But the more you do it, the more likely it becomes that something creative will happen. It's an unwritten contract between you and whatever else is out there. Show up, put in the work, and maybe a godly experience will be the reward."

I got a chuckle out of Steve when I asked him if integrity was some sort of moving goalpost in the game of "Fake it til you make it" as an improviser.

SD: "Confidence is so important in improvising. If it comes from a place of genuine vulnerability to the process, I think it is more likely to be worthwhile. When you're just starting out, there's an expectation that you have to sound a certain way to get people to listen to you. Conversely, people can sort of hear that in our playing. The belief that we're not really good enough to be listened to comes from society's expectation, and has very little to do with the qualities of our sound.

"I had an interesting experience recently. I was substitute teaching an improvisation class for a friend of mine. I had never met these kids before. I think they were mostly around ten years old. The younger group, which I remember was between six and three, were just happy to be playing anything, but the older group was much more reserved. It was as if the notion of playing music to have fun was just off the table. So I asked the older kids what was going on, and they told me it was different for them because now they knew what it was like to feel embarrassed.

"I definitely had that as a kid. I was shy, and it felt awkward to play in front of other people because having fun was no longer as important as being good. The word we most often associate with making music is "play," but playing as a child, like shredding on an air guitar, is valued less than having skill. There is value in having technique, in understanding some music theory. They are all important building blocks, but the essence is playing—taking whatever is in front of you at the moment and making art with it."

Our conversation stumbled for a second as we tried to ascribe the concept of expertise being a return to innocence, to a particular experiential setting.. We were pretty sure we both read it in Twyla Tharp's book *The Creative Habit: Learn it and Use It for Life*, but weren't sure if it was Picasso, or Hemingway who deserved the credit. The tangent of a return to innocence being a driving force in the search for salvation seemed to beg for a musical catalogue. The joy in listening, or playing, could well be the differentiation of a piece of music being merely a cultural phenomenon or a spiritual, even supernatural, experience. Some sort of connective tissue to the soul is what appears to make certain organized sounds larger than life.

Steve mentioned playing in a wedding/bar band for seven years, which was a great formative experience for learning to play danceable music. But the experience of playing with Marian Hill reflected a different type of feedback from the audience that led Steve to desire greater connection with the band members and the audience.

> *SD: I kind of feel as if connection is more of a mind set. If I'm enjoying playing music with a group of people, the audience response is almost secondary. In the dance band, we added a trumpet player and a trombonist. I started really listening to the music in a way I hadn't*

before, maybe it was a Stevie Wonder tune, and I realized, "This is a really good tune!" And it changed my energy to the point where I knew I was putting out all the good energy I could into the piece. If people wanted to just sit at the bar instead of dance, there really wasn't much I could do to change the situation.

Just two days ago Marian Hill and I were playing a festival in Austin. A guy came up to us as we were packing and said, "I really enjoyed your music tonight. I never heard of you before, but I want to check you out. Do you have any recordings?"

It was a reminder that even the stuff we're used to playing can be fresh for the first-time listener. For lack of a better term, the more expressive music I'm involved in making is sometimes more of a thrill for the performers than the audience, but my experience is that once someone's been exposed to that type of music, the free improvisational stuff, they more willing to hear more of it.

When we work with children, there's a leap from worrying about getting it right to make music that is a shared reward, that's interesting as more than just a process. The constant balance is between creating something that satisfies myself as an artist and creating something that resonates with other people. On the one hand the music industry is all about entertainment which, let's face it, can become sort of shallow, but then again, if my art is entirely self-serving, it becomes less effective as a means of communication.

What people want from us when we're performing is just to hear us play. They don't want to be pandered to. It's a tricky balance. I want to create something that I can believe in, something that's worth my time and the audience's time. Time, and attention, are our most precious things to share—just look at how much of it we squander on trivial things. Putting another person's expectations and values into my artistic perspective is something I'm constantly playing around with, but I can't be thinking about that when I'm playing because it would interrupt the creative flow.

Being a professional musician, it's still pretty easy to get distracted by all the shiny and bright attraction of being popular. The switch in my head was when I realized writing songs, making the actual music is what I enjoyed the most. When some of what I produced began to click with other people, I got tempted to pursue people's response to my music, and I nearly lost the purpose of it again. The obligation to be creative, to be productive, creates this mirage that obstructs the actual work."

CHAPTER SEVEN

Have I Mentioned My Mentor?

♪♪♪

I had long hoped to meet up again with my maestro, Tony Pagano, and play some music together. In the mid '90s, on a trip to New York, we had arranged via telephone to hook up, but he took a paying job in Boston that night, and I lost track of him for another twenty years. I learned that he moved back to France. Using all my internet skill, I found a website that offered information of his recent bookings and recordings. I ordered all three of his CDs without worrying what the conversion rate of Euros to dollars might be. Within a few weeks, I had Tony's sound back in my heart.

The website had an email address, and I sent a personal note to Tony with a short video attachment of me playing the melody to "Goodbye Pork Pie Hat" on my alto. He replied that it was good to hear from me and that I had a good tone on the alto. For the next decade or so, I fantasized about getting to Europe to hear him play in person and hopefully to get another life lesson from my hero. His first lesson to me back in 1974 was to find a way to be wealthy so I could play what I want where and when I want. I can't say I transposed that into actual fact.

As the notion of writing this book began to gain traction, I mused how terrific it would be to get to France and interview Tony as the culmination of the whole project. However, no amount of internet scrolling brought me any closer to the dream until one day my bride and I found an obscure French music site that listed Tony as an instructor at a mountainside music retreat. This was it! A dream come true!

I noted the date 7-4-2018 and began to seriously daydream about arriving at the workshop and playing "Will the Circle Be Unbroken" as I walked into the auditorium. The reality of European date notation burst my bubble when we realized the date of the conference was in April, two days away, not in July. I laughed about it and emailed the conference coordinator that I would not be able to make it.

A few months went by with no news until a pianist who recorded with Tony informed me that Tony had likely passed away later that spring in his early '80s. I never found an obituary in either the French or Philadelphia press.

I played his CDs over and over again, recalling lessons, gigs, and meals we shared. I remembered how we teamed up to do a poetry/jazz show in Milwaukee May 8, 1978 at Century Hall for about 200 people after the local poetry bar wouldn't give me a date. And another time we played for the ducks and geese at the local water park, which eventually drew the attention of the park security detail. But the most vivid memory I had was watching Tony in a tuxedo playing a Christmas concert for Midwestern highbrows.

Tony spoke to me about coming into a piece as the lone saxophone on a low C#, as a combination of the softness of the first daffodil of spring braving a late snowfall and the ring of an elite officer's sword unleashed from a jeweled scabbard. As a beginning student, my concept of playing that note was limited to holding a weird key down with my pinkie and hoping I had enough air to reach the bottom of the bell. Clearly worlds apart in our approach and appreciation of a difficult fingering and articulation, we were yet joined by virtue of the journey.

When I heard Tony perform the piece, he had sneaked me into the concert hall by giving me an instrument case to carry in through the stage door, the opening note cut through the sound of the entire orchestra. Yet, somehow it didn't draw attention to itself but laced the mood and textures of sound together. It's been forty years since I heard that concert. I can't tell you what the piece was or any other facet of the performance, but I can still hear that C# and picture the whole setting from my stowaway's seat in the balcony.

I wrote a poem about a time I heard Tony play at a red-bricked jazz club, under a freeway, in Milwaukee. The junior trumpet player in the poem is Bryan Lynch, who went on to play with Abby Lincoln, Phil Woods, The Jazz Messengers and

Horace Silver. I don't remember the name of the trombonist.

Street level windows reflect the red chrysanthemums
of haloed radio towers while piano
lounge lights wash the river.
The band is between sets,
smoke in the alley climbs the brick wall
floats angelic in a search for wings.

The overpass carries cars to some other music, jazz,
being an acquired culture, leaves room
for parking. The midnight encore
of last call brings the drummer
back to the throne.

Three horns come to the mic
in one voice, thirty years between them
and the chart. The chorus catches light
on the spot and trills to the tip
of an ice cube melting
in a neglected glass.

Study this to know how eternity breathes;.
the romance of exiting by the same door
to a night of alone together humming
in the street. The trumpet player,
being junior, pockets twenty bucks
for the night, packs his case.

Tuesday takes its place
in the memory of music made
in America. Instruments
of peace fit in the trunks
of Pontiacs and Chevrolets
sliding toward the freeway.

The stuff on the radio
is what folks know.
The sound of tires on the road
thrums the heartland home.
By the time the stars catch the beat
the song will rival a dream.

♪ ♪ ♪

My imagination confirms if you wet your finger and circle the lip rim of the Holy Grail with just enough finesse, you'll get something similar to Tony's C#. I am certain the rungs on Jacob's Ladder are tuned to musical scales. Obviously the celestial winds don't only blow in western tunings. I can probably thank George Harrison's sitar work for demonstrating that while I was in high school. Yet, I take heart in stories of cross-cultural connection being made by adapting keys. The banjo player Abigail Washburn recounts in an online conversation published in *On Being* that while traveling in China, she met a traditional erhu player—an erhu is a two-stringed instrument likened to a violin. He lamented the dissonance between American and Chinese cultures.

Upon hearing the man play, her band mates tuned up their instruments to play along. Happy with their blend into a Tibetan melody, they incorporated the song into the evening's performance. The townspeople, and the erhu player, rejoiced in the collaboration of unexpected harmonies of the heart. Abigail explained that songs become containers for empathy. Carrying a tune creates handles on the wheelbarrow of the world. We lessen each other's loads by listening and by chiming in appropriately. Harmony is not reserved for the gifted, but is honed by those with an ear for adaptability.

Does what or who we hear carry us? Or is it the other way around? The power of pop tunes to completely fill our heads is the penultimate puzzle of Zen Koans slapping a bear in the woods. The still, small voice of my grandson playing a finger cymbal, in time, during his first-grade recital is a genuine link to my soul's ear that the world's streaming will never know.

I am so out of the loop of current culture that I can recognize more names in the memoriam list than in the Grammy nominees. I strive to keep a treasure alive in my listening, and playing, that springs from a well we won't miss until it runs dry.

Improvisational music improves our lives. When we kick out the jams, we open a channel of creativity too often delegated to the professionals. We can always get better at making music, connections, and friends. Perfect practice makes perfect sense, but being an amateur is just another way of spelling "student of life." Music is too human and too divine to assign away like a dream we try to shake with morning coffee. There is inherent value in row, row, rowing our boats gently down the stream.

I've had more time to practice this week than most, and the physical familiarity with my instrument is a welcome change from repeatedly starting over from scratch. It dawned on me the folks who meditate, or at least practice mindfulness, say they have a similar experience within their own bodies, a sort of operator's confidence. I'm hoping to experience some sort of corollary in my real life from improvement as an instrumentalist.

Perhaps it's too much to hope for; yet overcoming self doubt and graduating up the levels of technical appropriation seems a basic foundation of learning to live a contented life. Could the mental health factor of learning to play an instrument well be an as yet unseen reason to increase the profile of music, and music appreciation, in our school's curriculums? I sometimes daydream of a video world where matching melodies to dancing baselines would be as popular as blowing shit up.

One technique I have long resisted under the excuse that it was only for real musicians, is transcribing music by ear from recordings to my instrument. The breakthrough came when I realized if I could whistle the tune, I could probably search out the notes on my horn and approximate the rhythms. My teachers all said, "Sing it first," which left me ample room to balk. But whistling, which I inherited from my father, suddenly gave me a confident access to musical mimicry.

Every mentor, teacher, or compatriot in this process of becoming a progressing musician has encouraged me to "be my own teacher," which always struck me as counterintuitive because, after all, what did I know about playing music? The hidden-in-plain sight lesson reveals a foundation of fundamental development. The time, conscious, or semi-conscious we spend listening to music, or matching bird whistles if you're an ornithologist, creates recognition habits that can assist in playing patterns to an instrument. The moment I realized I could match the notes I made whistling to notes on my horn, well let's just say I came late to the party, but I'm headed straight to the chip bowl to dip into the tunes circulating around me.

Maybe I could rephrase that: I'm headed to the piano I just bought, to plunk the notes of a tune on the radio out of thin, but thinking, air. I mention I just bought the keyboard in the hopes I can write off the purchase once this book comes out. My momma didn't raise no dummies, except for me and my brothers—and my brother turned me onto to listening to jazz.

I heard some live jazz just last night—Charles McPherson Quartet with Billy Drummond, Jeb Patton, and Jeff Littleton at the local college. My brother couldn't make it, so I traded his ticket for coffee and cookies and took my seat in the fourth row.

He would have felt right at home in the crowd of aging hipsters. Out of a crowd of two hundred people, I counted maybe a dozen under the age of fifty—and that included the band. A live jazz concert at a university of eight thousand or so students, including a music department, was represented by maybe six music students. Judging by their enthusiasm, and slouching backpacks, I would say the kids enjoyed the gift of living legends playing live improvisational music, even if it was bebop.

I sat up in my seat as the band suddenly came out from behind the stage curtain and took their place. The band's body language began to sing before they sounded a single note. Even standing still they seemed to already be humming together. McPherson counted off in that magic, whisper tone reserved for bandleaders, and the music began shaping the future.

The way he held his horn reminded me of Joe Henderson's posture, who I incidentally heard at a different campus performance back when I was in the student section. The horn was locked in place at the loose end of his arms. One position for slow ballads, same position for blistering workhorse renditions of Cherokee and Tenor Madness. The fingers, not the shoulders, moved the melody along. The air chambers of lungs, throat, and *embouchure* were never pinched or impeded. The years and years of steady, studied progress trimmed his body's response to the demands of the tune to the absolute.

He dipped lightly to one side, maybe more as a cue to the audience to get ready for the high altissimo notes than any physical necessity. Then he wielded the awkward side palm keys like Picasso swirled a brush. I watched him play the horn as intently as I could to affix the mechanics of it in my memory bank. However, I had to close my eyes to believe all this musical construction and articulation was emanating from the slightly framed warrior in the billowing white Nehru shirt.

The pianist's elbows winged above his flying fingers as if they were part of some large bellows forcing the harmonic flames into dancing peaks and then hissing quietly as settled embers. From the angle of my seat, I could just make out the drummer's face between the flashing cymbals, and I witnessed something so commonplace, and yet extraordinary, that it struck me like a rim shot on his snare. He was looking at the other musicians, making eye contact, insisting, pleading, and proving each beat, and micro beat, was to support the music, to move the band. It seemed clear, to me at least, he was playing for the music, for the band, and to the audience.

The bassist, as expected, stitched all the fabrics of sound together into a full-blown sail. He occasionally led the charge, like a banner going into battle, or waving at other points in the continually moving story, like a flag planted on the moon. The chamber room boomed heart-to-heart, breath-to-breath as what we understood to be music became sensation, sound, and a spirited shared direction to an inner experience. The concerted effort of years of study, performance, and modulation proved the timelessness is what makes the rhythm of life become a dance in the place of drudgery. The triumph of live jazz is unbelievably accumulated by listening to the bone.

CHAPTER EIGHT

Coda

♫♫♫

It was my good fortune to be informed of the McPherson concert by word of mouth, specifically the mouth of an English professor, David Stacey who plays trumpet in a rehearsal band I have been sitting in with over the last year. I am compelled to expound on what a miracle that last sentence contains.

My day job is delivering packages to businesses and consumers. I learned, during COVD-19, that I am considered essential for doing this, which is a bit humbling for my rotating poet-author-musician hats to handle. One day, while admiring the garden sprouting along a client's driveway, I got into a conversation with the recipient of the cardboard mystery I dropped on his porch. I introduced myself as a poet, in case this person ever needed one.

Harry Smith, the gardener, then introduced himself as a pianist, in case I ever needed one. Exclaiming that I was also a saxophonist and certainly did need a pianist got me a tour of Harry's living room which housed a stand up and baby grand piano as well as a set of drums. Harry, and his bride, Sherry, regularly practiced tunes from the *Great American Songbook*, and I was invited to come back on a Friday morning with my horn and jam with the house band.

At this point in my musical history, I can count on one hand the times I've jammed with credible jazz musicians outside of sax camp. I explain I barely read music but am willing to learn, and the date is set for me to sit in with the songsmiths the next Friday at 10:00 a.m.

Harry proves to be a very encouraging and patient individual, and before long the notion of finding my way around a personal list of tunes begins to take shape. I don't always hold my place in the chord progressions, but gradually I make up coherent solos and can duplicate the heads from the volumes of *Real Books* stacked next to Harry's piano. Within a few months, Harry invited a bass player, also named Smith, and David Stacey, the trumpeter, to round out our Friday morning group. For the first time in my life, after forty years of private woodshedding, I have a musical context for studying and playing music that involves having living human beings in the same room.

It's an answer to a prayer I hadn't realized I was praying, which is of course the richest kind. I began to find my place in the tradition. Every week I came to play and came away either more confident, or confounded, depending on the material at hand.

One day it dawned on me that jazz chord symbols are sometimes longer in print than the actual passing chords in the melody. The G minor with a flat 5 shifting to a C dominant with a flat 9 is for all purposes only the difference of changing one note by a half step (excluding the root of the dominant).

The chords have more notes in common than not, and after decades of supposing jazz chords were purposefully made difficult to out egghead the classical musicians, I saw—in black and white keys—

that the simplicity of a chord change is part of the legitimacy of jazz theory. The "voicing" of the chords gives the music its inherent and interpretive meaning. Talk about epiphanies! The next steps I embarked on in my journey to becoming a better jazz musician/student had the markings of a road mapped out in front of me and like many a disciple before me, I had but to heed the call to follow.

Had I not been a willing enough student before to make the teacher appear? I can't quite answer that; it does seem that every ten years or so a connection to other musicians has lined up for me to keep me stumbling forward. The joke about learning to walk on water is to know where the flat rocks are in the stream. To know where the notes are in the song, to know where the chords lay in the rhythm of the tune, is part of knowing where the masters stand in the history of the music.

For me to know where God is in the mix, in the midst of creative collaboration, is the sub plot, the sub tone of making music, or should I say letting music make me a better person? Listening, feeling, expressing are the essentials of communication.

Finding a common grounding in shared flights of fancy riffs and centric rhythms is a basic tribal component that technology is more likely to enhance than obliterate. The scriptural premise of, Be still and know I AM God has a B-side, God Make Me Funky is a prayer for our times.

To be consciously aware of both a Super consciousness, and a subconscious foundation is how we might count ourselves into the song of life. Music is available to address our every human emotion, linking it to a devotional sense of well being in harmony with a Very Well Being is perhaps a clue to composing ourselves as a compassionate, planet saving society.

I am honored to have spoken with the dozens of musicians who contributed to this book and I hope I have done some justice to their insights and enthusiasm. Music, much like matters of faith, is too important to leave to the professionals. We are the World is a song as much as an operating political principle. The Sound of Spirit may be any sound that moves us; a rushing wind, the crashing surf, but the organized sounds we make together, or alone, are our testimony.

You don't have to be a Holy Rolling Southern Baptist to have a testimony. The dictionary defines the term as pertaining to as evidence in support of a fact, but for the purposes of this book it may point more towards individual, or group experience and therefore subject, like jazz, to interpretation. In my efforts to encourage your own testimony let me share a case in point.

♫ ♫ ♫

Previous to the Covid 19 pandemic I had hoped to interview a local musician I've had the pleasure of listening to since I relocated to Humboldt County in northern California. Tim Randles is a very fine and funky pianist whose Bossa Nova style lends sway and influence to every outdoor festival of note in these parts. Tim is also a practitioner and teacher of the same Tai Chi style I practice,(the Yang style of Chien Man-Ching) and has been instructing senior citizens in the meditative movement for better than twenty years.

Tim teaches piano, primarily to youngsters, and I have taken a few classes with him to the amazement of the eight to ten year olds who realize I'm not at the studio to pick up a student but am harboring hopes of becoming one. In lieu of a face to face interview I decided to play with Tim's Zen take on the depths of improvisational potential and ask him for a few paragraphs on the sound of one hand vamping in the rainforest and this is what he offers on the subject of free play.

>TR: *"It is believed by some that there is no smallest particle in the Universe. That as we delve deeper and deeper, we are confronted not by a final infinitesimal monad: but by infinity itself. It's as if matter sends out invisible roots that sink forever into an endless energy. There is no way we can ever comprehend intellectually a concept like this; the only way it can possibly be perceived, is by feeling.*
>
>*I have been playing piano ever since my mother brought a spinet into our small apartment when I was eight years old. Almost instantly, I became entranced with spontaneous play; I would become lost its variety of colors.*

Though try as I might, I could never become comfortable with my classical studies; but I was always at ease when no particular notes needed to be played.

I am now sixty-seven, with much experience behind me. For the last three years, I have done two-hour sessions, three days a week, with my next-door neighbor, an internationally renowned jazz violinist. When she is not touring, she engages me as a sort of "rehearsal pianist" to keep herself in shape, until she flies off to play with some of the best musicians in the world. Much of our time is spent devising drills with modes and arpeggios, rhythmic subdivisions, and whatever mental gymnastics we can come up with to stretch out our musical limits. There is so much to be learned from being around a world-class musician.

But what we enjoy doing beyond anything else, is just to play, with no boundaries. Any of the twelve notes is fair game. During these periods of complete musical freedom, I tend to lose myself and let go of my control, allowing the music to play itself however it pleases. The music becomes more of a direct experience: a feeling.

We as human beings are part of the great potential of the universe. We are it's sense organs, and we are the tools through which the universe can manifest it's limitless potential. So as I, part of this great universe, am drawing out these unusual combinations of notes, it feels to me, to be an expression of that infinite energy to which all matter is rooted."

🎵🎵🎵

If you listen closely, you might be able to hear my testimony rehearsing in the distance. Once the pandemic is favorably resolved, I resolve to take my music to the next level and sign up for a tune or two at the local jam session—the friendly one for students and seniors at the Sunday afternoon coffee bar, not the professional two-drink minimum Tuesday night at The Speak Easy where Tim is the house pianist.

It's time for me to test the theory that music theory is merely preparation for the real thing of improvising. My coaches tell me to apply the same sincerity to music that I engage when writing poetry. Just last week, I attempted to add some blues lines to a spoken word piece we're recording for an EP project (*Fix My Car* recorded at Noble House Studio in Arcata, Calif.) I got a little too excited, too caught up in the thrill of being in a studio again after nearly twenty years.

It didn't go particularly well, but not particularly awful either. I proved not practicing for a week and warming up for less than five minutes guarantees a certain result. But even in that, a prayer was answered. I had a moment when my horn absolutely supported the emotion and the context of the poem "God Walks Into a Twelve Bar Blues." There's room for improvement and that, my friends, is why we improvise. Things can always get better.

There is a song inside each of us that insists this is so. Music can and will answer the call to pay attention, to pay homage, to pay it forward. The sound that you're hearing might be the low spark of high-heeled boys, or it might be your name translated into beats and arpeggios. The sound of my spirit might be in counterpoint to yours, or it could be an abstract notion like playing a reel-to-reel recording backwards to simulate artificial rain.

Our breath is air moving into our lungs; our music is spirit moving out into the air. When we're learning to read, our parents and teachers ask us to sound out the difficult words.

Imagine a world where singing out the difficult and the glorious could indeed be part of our universal language. You don't have to be John Lennon to get it to come together; you don't have to be trained, proficient, or even own an instrument. Regrets are prevented, unseated, by starting with a whole, or half step of faith towards the goal of whatever we always wanted to do. Sew a pillow, write a book, take a solo, The Creator does have a Master Plan, and you're part of it. No tags back.

God Walks Into a Twelve Bar Blues

The melody is out of our hands.
Only the black keys cast a shadow.
The moon warms to center stage,
Blues night packs the house.

Waiting for the chorus,
in a backlit row of clamor,
half notes lengthen
the span of attention.

The tune carries weight
and the star of the show points north
reflecting promise selling
the future.

A solo is never finished alone.
Not just the drum, but the skin
stretches to the limit
of our pulsing heart.

We take to the tip jar
like a conga line to bread and wine,
dipping our fingers spoon deep
into the high crashing symbol.

This church, keyed up in neon,
revives in thunder. What we name
takes a bow, encourages
an encore.

ENDNOTES

The following individuals were interviewed by the author at various times and places. Their permission for use of these interviews is in the personal files of the author.

Pgs. 44-50	Russ Paladino, saxophonist
Pgs. 52-58	Mario Scaramuzza, saxophonist
Pgs. 68-70	Herman Sosa, saxophonist
Pg. 71	Thieme Schipper, saxophonist
Pgs. 75-80	Steve Clark, Musician, Lifehouse Church, Humboldt County, California
Pgs. 84-91	Joel Valle, instrumentalist & musical coach
Pgs. 95-102	Naoko Rivera, musician
Pgs 103-114	Noah Watkins, musician
Pgs. 116-126	Justin Grimaldo, musician
Pgs. 154-159	Selina Wesley, The House of Refuge Christian Fellowship choir director, Santa Rosa, California
Pgs 166-167	Haley Gurr, Praise Singer

Pgs. 170-178	Bob Franceschini, Inside Out Retreat founder, Musician
Pgs. 179-181	Bob Hemenger, Inside Out Retreat founder, Musician
Pgs. 182-188	Bob Reynolds, Inside Out Retreat founder, Musician
Pgs. 189-192	Mary Hendershott, musician,
Pgs. 193-198	Juan Carlos Rollan, musician
Pgs. 199-205	Steve Davit, musician
Pgs 225-226	Tim Randles, musician

ALSO BY THE AUTHOR

♪♪♪

Jesus Inside A Prison Minister's Memoir and Training Manual

Head Lines Poems & Provocations

Both available by request wherever books are sold or online at Barnes&Noble, BAM, Walmart. Signed copies of these books are available on Will's website at www.schmitbooks.com

♪♪♪

Music from Will's CD, *Bring to Glory*, is available to stream at Spotify, iTunes or download at schmitbooks.com (Hard copies are sold out)

Also available are tunes from Will's new EP, *Fix My Car* (signed discs are available at the above website).

www.ingramcontent.com/pod-product-compliance
Lightning Source LLC
Chambersburg PA
CBHW030148100526
44592CB00009B/175